The Undefended Life

Rediscovering God's Freedom

to Live Beyond Fear

Simon P. Walker

The Undefended Life

First published in Great Britain in 2011

Text and graphics by Simon P. Walker

Copyright (c) Simon P. Walker

ISBN: 978-1-907459-03-0

Human Ecology Partners

Cover design by Simple Faith Creative

For those who are travelling home

Contents

Part III The Quest for the Good Life: Seven contemporary aspirational pathways

About the author

Simon Walker is author of seven books and now teaches adults how to develop as undefended leaders. An ordained priest in the Church of England, he completed a research degree studying applied psychology and went on to develop a language around human flourishing which he has called Human Ecology.

He pioneered the Undefended Leader course at Wycliffe Hall, Oxford University, in the UK in 2002, through which a growing number of Christian leaders around the world have now been trained. He now travels widely, particularly to Africa and Asia, to support leaders seeking to live out what it means to be undefended in life and work.

Simon's company, Human Ecology, also works successfully in the corporate space transforming both leaders and business practice.

Author's Preface

I have written this book in large part as a way of honouring those people who have travelled on this journey with me over the past eight years. Specifically, there is a group of some five hundred or so who have participated in some version of The Undefended Leader course. Whilst, ostensibly, we have been exploring leadership, the heartbeat of our travels has actually been to find an undefended way of living in the world.

Amongst the thirty of so course groups I can recall so many moments of deep, extraordinary healing, as well as recovery and freedom. I have watched people learn how to listen to each other, how to hold each others' stories, how to become still and join in the movements of God. I have witnessed the most moving and powerful redemptive encounters and have been given the privilege of playing some part in those stories.

I offer these people, and all readers, this book in the hope that it may continue to provide an open doorway deeper into the life and the divine community, Father, Son and Spirit. It is the theology they have been waiting for, the vocabulary they have been reaching for.

Many people have been involved in honing this text along the way. Anna Cuccio gave invaluable editorial input which shaped the manuscript. Adam Chapman and Mark Powley both reviewed the theological statements I was making and their comments informed the final version. At Berit, Robert and Philip gave their full and unconditional backing to the project, enabling the project to take off.

Originally much of this manuscript was released on my blog website through weekly chapter releases throughout the summer of 2010. I would like to express my appreciation to all those who made the effort to read and comment on the chapters as they emerged. My hope is that they will appreciate this completed and bound edition even more than the draft version they read staring at a screen for hours on end!

Introduction

Why Be Undefended Anyway?

"Maturity is the freedom to live and undefended life.'"
att. Melanie Kline

'Maturity is the freedom to live an undefended life.' Hearing that sentence was for me one of those puncturing moments in life. I remember exactly where I was when I heard it, just as many can recall where they were when they heard the news of the shooting of JFK on 22nd June 1963. These are moments which, for whatever reason, break into our reality in such an abrupt and rupturing way that the fabric of our narrative always retains the tear.

I was standing in our church lobby, talking to my senior colleague, a vicar in a church as it happened. We had finished our weekly staff meeting and were in a general way discussing our favourite pastoral topic—why people behave the way they do and how to help them grow in their faith. Geoff was one who always had, through his life and ministry, the wisdom and depth to seek for fuller understandings of the human condition than most others attempt. It was not uncommon for him to drop into conversation some quotation or idea from his avid reading which made me and others sit up. When he said this particular quotation, it was like he had set a small time bomb ticking inside me which, although I did not know it then, would fizzle away and finally detonate twelve years later.

What gripped me in the guts instantly, when I first heard those words, was a visceral realisation that I myself was not mature. It was not that I reflected on the truth of the statement and later concluded that I was probably somewhat defended. No: I simply knew, somewhere within me, that the term 'undefended' did not apply to me. I knew, in my guts, that Simon Walker was a person with locked rooms inside and walls around him.

At the same moment, I also knew another thing: I wanted more than anything to know what it meant to be undefended.

Defending ourselves has to do with threat, and threat results in fear. Whilst I could identify that I was defended, it was less easy for me to pinpoint exactly what I was afraid. Fear is a funny thing. We are not often 'greatly afraid', as we are told the shepherds were when they encountered the multitude of the heavenly host. I cannot recall the last time I was conscious of being physically threatened or fearing for my life. Fear is much more like a hidden stream that flows under our depths, rarely surfacing into the light of day. We can go for long periods of our lives barely acknowledging its existence. We can build landscapes of apparent calm and even tranquillity. Even those of us who have sunk boreholes down to investigate our subterranean realities are only partially aware of the dark routes the river flows along, or the source from which it originates.

The way fear manifests itself to us is more like a pervasive leaching out through the soil. A condition that is, somehow, always with us but mostly unrecognised. For some people, fear is present as a pervasive, low-level anxiety—an uncertainty about life. It is the emotion which lies underneath the slight dread of the day ahead, the sinking feeling at going back to work, the gloom that settles over one facing the prospects of the future. The dark conjuror that casts the veil over our reality, rendering us unable to appreciate the sunlight beyond.

Or, for others, fear is a hard master, controlling our thoughts, or demanding hours of our life attending to his needs: the gnawing worry about our finances that creeps into our thoughts at every corner of the day, or the apparently endless turning over of our concerns and prospects. It is the slightly obsessive planning, rehearsing and improving, making sure that everything is as well-thought through as possible, that nothing can go wrong, or trip us up.

For others still, fear is a hidden thief, a returning burglar who breaks into one's storehouse of joy and slyly removes our treasures: the anxiety of our loved ones getting ill, our business failing, losing our job, a relationship breaking, an unexpected tragedy. Despite our best efforts to build a happy and secure life, no lock or bolt seems strong enough to keep out the heartless intruder who will slip back inside and plunder our carefully amassed goods.

For others, fear is an unpassable giant bestriding the road to new choices, blocking the path ahead. Applying for a new job become unthinkable, moving house becomes too daunting, proposing to your fiancée becomes an impossible risk, confronting an aggressive boss terrifying. Fear traps us in a limited world, with 'No Entry' signs down many of the paths that once might have been open.

Fear is a dark conjuror casting a veil over reality. Fear is a hard task master demanding our attention. Fear is a sly thief robbing us of treasure. Fear is a vast giant blocking our pathways to change. However fear resides within us, the impact of fear is always the same. We are left diminished by its presence, reduced from the people we could be.

Perhaps one of the reasons most of us do not wage a more aggressive campaign to rout fear from our lives is that we feel largely impotent in the face of its forces. After all, how do you begin to tackle something so pervasive, so slippery, so largely invisible? We do better with other emotional conflicts. Guilt, for example. In general, we can identify why we feel guilty. Having found the source (that act which hurt another or that thing we wish we had not done), we can do something about it. Confess, apologise, ask for forgiveness and, quite possibly, receive an absolution. Of course, those guilty thoughts might return, but rarely do they pervade our whole being in the way that fear does.

Anger is an emotion that gets the better of many people. Anger can be deeply destructive, threatening so much in our lives. Anger, like fear, can also be difficult to root out of our lives. Perhaps one of the reasons for this is that, as psychologists increasingly suggest, anger grows out of fear. In other words, expressing anger is one response we may have to being afraid.

Later in the book, I write about the work my wife has done as a professional behavioural counsellor in schools. So often the aggressive teenage lads who terrorise pupils and staff alike will confess to their actions as a way of coping with being deeply afraid. When we are threatened, our response is to either fly or fight. They choose the latter.

Perhaps that is why some of our attempts to deal with our anger fail. We are dealing with the wrong issue—the symptom rather than the disease. In my own life, I have come to recognise that, behind many behaviours I manifest, lies a more general condition of fear. In my teens, I was a high achiever at school and university. I had a drive to excel. Why? Why was I so performance-orientated? Why had I come to experience the sensation of pleasure only when I exceeded expectations? In truth, the answer lay in a hardly visible fear that, unless I achieved, then those I respected and whose opinions I valued would judge and condemn me.

In my twenties, I slipped into a sequence of increasingly deep and prolonged cycles of depression. I noticed that these would coincide with being about two years into a job. Why? Why was I so fragile and prone to depression when the quality of my work was high, people were pleased with me, and things seemed to be going well? In truth, the answer lay in the fact that, by now, I really was not very much impacted by the opinions of others. I myself had become the 'judgmental audience', observing my own performance, and I now set myself my own internal standards. What was happening was that I would clear the bar of my own personal expectations in a job, only then to set it higher in order to prove to myself that I was still excelling. Gradually, over a couple of years, the bar got higher and higher until, as I looked at it, I started to worry that I was not able to find the energy, strength or skill to jump over it again. At that point, I started to become depressed.

Later on, I came to realise that my depressions were not sadness at falling short, but rather dark retreats into which I could withdraw from the threat of rejection. Depression was, for me, a medical state which finally gave me a get-out clause from the high jump competition. If I was clinically depressed then I could not be expected to take part in the competition any more, could I? Knocking the bar off was okay. I vividly remember the relief at being formally diagnosed as suffering from 'depression' by the doctor. It was my only way out. Whilst I did not have the maturity to choose a way out consciously, my unconscious devised one for me.

Once again, fear had taken its pound of flesh, this time casting a decade of my life in a pall of grey. But it was not finished with me yet. My exit from cycles of depression came, in part, from realising that I could choose not to be. The grip of those external and internal judges no longer had any power over me, and failing was a threat hanging over me no longer. This sparked a new season, in my thirties, of freedom and abundance out of which many good things grew. However, there lay a yet deeper stream of fear running under my subsoil and it was only after several more years that I became aware that its toxicity was still poisoning my life.

My children were now older and my two boys approaching secondary school. My work had taken me into a deeper study of the prospects of the Western economy and I found myself increasingly gloomy about the economic state of the world my children would inherit. I found myself doubting their ability to succeed in such a harsh environment. I doubted they would have the opportunities I myself had been afforded and increasingly felt it would be up to me to continue to provide for them in some shape or form.

This placed on me unsustainable financial pressure. I was gripped by worry and became preoccupied with the markets and finding strategies to invest wisely. The fear robbed me and my family of much time and energy as I scowled and growled endlessly about how much pressure was on me to work for their needs.

As my humour and warm relationship with my boys was increasingly stolen, so my actual pocket was also picked by fear. Investing desperately, I lost a large amount of our family savings.

I could almost hear the chuckles of the thief of fear as he won, crushing me in his victory. Those weeks of my life revealed to me just how powerful that grip of fear truly can be and how he is quite capable, and willing, to squeeze the life out of any victim.

Fear is both immensely strong and extraordinarily subtle. He will not rear his head to be exposed if he can help it. Those who are conscious of actual fear dominating their lives are usually those so defeated and ravaged that they no longer have the capacity in themselves to recover from it. For most of us, fear is sly, avoiding outright confrontation, choosing to work through backdoors, masked and named as something else. So often he escapes our clutches by convincing us we are dealing with an alternative enemy—woundedness, guilt, pain, anger, pride, control, insecurity, vanity, ambition, etc. Fear is a master of disguise and we will not deal with any of the above without dealing with the tap root that lies underneath them. Uncloaking that archaeology of fear is one of the intents of this book.

'Maturity is the freedom to live an undefended life.' That quotation is attributed to Melanie Klein, an adherent of Freud, although the exact reference has alluded me. Klein's own understanding of that idea grew from her theory of the need for individuals securely to establish a proper sense of their own internal and external objects. Only when such objects (both the internal sense of self and also external relationships) were properly and securely established, could a person risk being isolated, alone, undefended. Klein, I believe, was right in appreciating that vulnerability is the deepest threat to a person, and that human maturation must deal with how an individual can suffer loss and vulnerability, and yet remain intact.

Ever since I embraced the Christian faith as my own at the age of thirteen I have been taught to believe that fullness of life can be found in that spirituality. I confess that I have known it myself only partially; yet the journey grips me, for I, like you, long to be free. I long to be fully alive. In reaching for this end, I have opened different and new doorways into the heart of the Christian Gospel. Some come from traditions outside that faith. Others come from rediscovering doorways which I, at least, had not known about or had forgotten, from ancient Christian paths long past. All, however, have opened up a space within that faith tradition which offers abundant life and freedom from fear.

What follows is an attempt to open up those doorways for others into what are, for many, familiar places. As we look with fresh eyes, perhaps, on old landscapes my hope is that others too will discover what I have come to believe is the very heart of God.

Part I
Locating Undefendedness
in the Gospel

Chapter 1

Beginning at the Beginning:
The Archetypal Fault Line

Love is what we were born with.

Fear is what we learned here.

(Anonymous)

Let us go back to an old story—one of the oldest there is—the story of creation and the fall in the first three chapters of the Book of Genesis. God creates a world and declares that it is good. In this world, he places Adam and Eve. Fundamentally, they experience this world as safe. It is safe on the basis of two conditions. First, God is for them. Second, God is all-powerful. Both of these conditions need to be met for Adam and Eve to be safe. If God were for them, but not all powerful, they would have been cared for but vulnerable; if God were all-powerful, but not for them, they would have been under threat.

It is no surprise, then, that the serpent begins to tease at one of those conditions. 'Is God really for you?', he questions, 'Really? If you look at it, God is not really for you—he's for himself. He's guarding his own status and privilege to knowledge and power. He doesn't want you to have what is his! He's not for you!' And at its heart, the archetypal sin of Adam and Eve, of mankind, is to choose to affirm that contention, to believe that God is NOT for them, to believe that God is not for us.

It is because of this choice that they eat the fruit—taking matters of their own welfare into their own hands. Now, here is a question: what is the first emotion they experience when they have eaten the fruit? Some of you think it is shame. Others think it is guilt. Others are reaching for their bible to discover that the first named emotion they experience upon eating the fruit, upon disobeying God, is, in fact, fear. They are afraid.

Why are they afraid?

Let's just think about it. They are afraid because God is no longer reliably for them. Having disobeyed God, they can no longer reliably predict that he is on their side. The second of those conditions is no longer met. God remains all-powerful, but he is no longer for them. Therefore, the world is no longer safe. Therefore, they are afraid.

Fear is the emotion we experience when we are unsafe. In the face of a threat, our amygdala releases adrenalin and cortisol. Adrenalin floods our body causing an array of physiological changes. Our pupils dilate; our hairs stand up on end; our heart rate increases; our palms sweat. Our bodies are getting ready for fight or flight. We are giving ourselves the best chance of survival we can. And safety is our basic human need. It is not our only human need; it is not even our deepest human need; but it is our most basic.

If you are standing in a road, with a car travelling at forty miles an hour, ten metres away from you, it does not matter how hungry you are, how lonely you are, how unfulfilled you feel; you get out of the way of the car. Safety takes precedence over any other need. If we cannot meet that need, then nothing else is relevant—we simply wouldn't be alive. That is why our threat-warning system is the shortest neural circuit we have in our brains. And it has worked well for us up to this point. It has needed to, because the experience of living in a world that is fundamentally and universally unsafe is the basic human experience.

This is the implication of the Genesis story—that the world we inhabit is now no longer safe. The choice that Adam and Eve make represents the archetypal fault line that exists in the world. God has created a world, but we have chosen to live in it as if he were not reliable or trustworthy. As a result, we no longer experience the world as a safe place, but rather as a threatening one. Managing danger is our chief preoccupation.

I want to tell you what your single most important achievement to date is in your life. I am sure many of you are highly successful, impressive individuals. Some of you may have hundreds of friends, or lead large organisations. Some of you have given birth, which I regard as the most courageous act I have ever witnessed! But, against all of these there is one achievement that is greater than all: it is that you are still alive to this day.

Think about it for a moment. The odds are not good. There is one of you, and there is six billion of them. Think about it. Your single, greatest achievement to date is to have lived, up to this moment, in such a way that you have avoided any one, or several, of those six billion people from turning against you. Neither you nor I would stand a chance if one hundred people concertedly wanted to be rid of us. I would not stand much chance against ten, or five, or perhaps even two. It would not take much to finish me off. But, you see, I have managed, and so have you, to avoid so upsetting anyone that they have wanted me rid of.

That is remarkable. It is a testament to the highly sophisticated behavioural skills I have developed. It is a remarkable testimony to your ability to detect danger and threat, and to get out of it. These skills enable you and me to negotiate dozens of social situations each day and achieve a relatively happy, benign outcome. And, if we take ourselves back to the Genesis story, we will see how early on these social skills developed to cope with an unsafe world.

Having eaten the fruit, and being now afraid, what do Adam and Eve do? They hide. They cover up. First, they stitch clothing together and, then, when God returns to the garden in the evening, they hide behind trees. Clothing is symbolic of hiding not just our bodies but also ourselves—protecting, concealing our vulnerabilities and intimacies, so they cannot be seen or exploited. The first way to cope with danger is, therefore, to protect ourselves, to cover up. Secondly, when they begin talking with God, he asks them what has happened. They tell him—or, at least, they give him a version of events. 'Well, I did eat the fruit, that's true, but it was only because the woman (who you gave me) made me.' 'Well, I did give it him, and eat it, but it was only because the serpent (whom you made) tempted me.' What's going on here is the business of trying to secure a less hostile response from God. God is still all powerful, but no longer reliably for them; they cannot afford for God to turn against them. Therefore, they have to secure a favourable response from him.

These are the origins of a universal strategy that humankind has used ever since to cope with an unsafe world: that strategy is the creation of a front stage and a back stage. The front stage is the version of ourselves that we present to the world, the version that generally secures a favourable response from the watching audience. The audience now is not just God, but also the rest of the population around us.

Once again, consider the figures: there is one of you and there are six billion others. You cannot afford an unfavourable response from this host of fellow habitants of this planet. Let us make it more local: imagine you go into a meeting at work. You have too much at stake to allow for people to leave the meeting with the impression that you are incompetent, rude or ill-prepared. That would, if repeated regularly, do great damage not just to your status but also your self-esteem. In fact, it does not matter what context you are thinking of—a project at work, a conversation at the school gate, a dinner party, talking to the neighbours, drinking coffee after church—few of us could cope with upsetting people and leaving them thinking badly of us. Probably, the last time we did this is seared on our memory.

All of us have developed a front stage—a version of ourselves that we present to the world. This may vary from context to context, but the point is that this self is very skilled at securing the favour of audiences. Now, of course, in order to do this, we have to hide away lots of things about ourselves. Depending on the audience, I may choose not to tell them about things that I know they would judge, disagree with, or be critical of. All these things that I cannot risk presenting have to be put somewhere. My back stage is the place I have learnt to put things that I do not want people to see. Some things I may be ashamed of; others may be broken or fragile; others may be precious or valuable things like ideas, thoughts, dreams, or feelings that I want to reserve for special, trusted people.

All of us have a front stage and all of us have a back stage. It is our primary way of keeping ourselves safe in an unsafe world. We are just like Adam and Eve.

Of course we are. The bible tells us that this story is not just a piece of history. It is a myth that dissects the fundamental axes of the world. The exploitation of the strategy of a front and back stage is not some optional idea that a few people have tried occasionally. It is the first and basic way we respond to the world as we find it. It is there in the bible. Being safe is our most basic human need. However, if the emotion of fear represents the biggest original fault line of fractured relationships, it is the emotion of guilt that tends to be more centrally addressed by the Church. Emphasis on the latter over the former emotion can prevent us from addressing the symptoms—namely the ways in which we cover up or cope with our fear.

The Guilt Narrative

Step back from this for a moment. Which would you say is the fundamental human emotion the Gospel is dealing with? I wonder if many of us, perhaps even most of us, would answer guilt (or possibly shame). Guilt is the predominant psychological and spiritual condition, which much of the Church's history has been concerned. The medieval practice of indulgences was a way of paying for the sins of one's forebears, whilst confession was the means of finding absolution from guilt now. Martin Luther's great realisation was St Paul's theology of justification through the atoning death of Jesus. The metaphor of justification—the judicial setting of a courtroom in which the condemned stands fairly convicted of their wrongdoing—is centrally about guilt.

The images of Jesus as the lamb of God taking away the sin of the world are mostly understood in terms of a removal, or carrying away, of guilt. And, of course, the chief blessing of the Gospel, as we tend to expound it, is the experience of forgiveness. 'Your sins are forgiven', pronounces Jesus to the crippled man lowered down through the roof . Forgiveness is that our sins will not be counted against us in the heavenly ledger. The slate is wiped clean, the balance paid off, and the price paid.

Orthodox theologians want to distinguish between guilt as an emotional state ('I feel guilty') and the judicial status of being found guilty of a crime or some wrongdoing ('I am guilty'). Jesus' atoning death, we assert, deals with the latter; this in turn should release us from the former. Of course, in reality, many followers of Jesus find this translation harder to make. Despite a cerebral knowledge, or strong belief, that they are no longer counted guilty in God's eyes, they struggle with a guilty conscience. Shame and guilt are strong imprints on our emotional memory and not easily erased.

One of the other features of the guilt narrative is it emphases the divine-human dimension of the fall, potentially at the expense of the human-human dimension. In the way we tend to understand it, each human being is guilty before God because none of us have lived up to His standards. We are all forensically guilty and therefore justly under judgement. This version of the Gospel relegates all of us to being perpetrators of an act, or acts, worthy of condemnation. Ultimately, it does not matter if I have been more violent than you, because, against the divine standard, we have both fallen disastrously short. The guilt narrative struggles to cope with the value of any act of human kindness or generosity, because it can neither atone for nor balance out the far greater acts that warrant condemnation. Hitler is condemned on the same score as the courageous, self-sacrificial but ultimately unbelieving Jewish prisoner of war of who gives their life so that a child might be spared.

But, guilt in the objective sense of having a guilty status is merely that: it is simply a statement that one is no longer in the right relationship with the other. If I am found guilty of stealing your car then I am no longer in a relationship with you in which I can be assured of your benevolence toward me. I have become to you an enemy because I have chosen to make you my enemy. Guilt is the means of formalising the status of a rupture within a trusting relationship and recognising that something must be done to put that breakdown right. Guilt points to the potential threat that has now emerged on the social horizon—the potential for violence to be done in return. This is what lies behind the provision in the Book of Joshua of the cities of refuge for those who accidentally kill someone . Before society can enact violence on them, they are given places of refuge where their objective status of guilt can be judged.

Guilt is a social expression of the breakdown of trust and freedom between the people concerned. It is the violence that flows from guilt that we need to recognise as significant. Guilt points to the looming shadow of threat now hanging over the society; it hints at the potential for unrest, retribution, aggression or revenge.

What lies behind the problem of guilt is the condition of threat; I am no longer safe in the world because I have acted in some way to undermine your safety. What I am suggesting is that the condition of guilt as highlighted in the bible leads us to reflect on the deeper, more primary condition of threat that exists from the Genesis story.

Guilt is a derivative of that story and points us back to it. Thus, we find that the subsequent story in Genesis 4 is one of violence in which Cain kills his brother Abel because Abel, in securing God's favourable response whilst Cain himself did not, became a threat to Cain.

The Fear Narrative

The condition of threat in which we experience the world, post-fall, as fundamentally and primarily unsafe suggests that the primary emotional condition, to which the Gospel will speak, is not guilt, but rather fear. God's movements in the world, by way of restoring his fallen world, must and will address the pathology of fear which spreads through relationships from generation to generation. The fear narrative opens up some potentially illuminating insights into familiar scriptural themes. Specifically, what are the means we employ to shore up our defences and how does God see them?

Idolatry

The second commandment is quite clear: God's people must not make for themselves an image of God and bow down to it . This instruction is much more than we sometimes take it for. It is more than a prohibition against depicting God's image in any visual way or against worshiping alternatives to God, such as money or family. An idol does encompass these things but it goes further. An idol is anything we look to for safety and protection other than God. The function of an idol is to give humans a sense of control in an uncertain world. This includes our own strategies to secure the favour of audiences.

To live in the ancient world was to live in a world with no predictable pattern to it. We find this difficult to appreciate. Several centuries of post-Newtonian physics have given us the illusion that our world is somehow run on principles or 'laws' which give us the ability to predict events with some degree of confidence. Notwithstanding that such an idea is, in itself, an illusion, the ancients had no such underpinning laws to their world. The harvest came, not because of seasonal rains but because the gods were favourable. The population increased in number because fecundity was blessed. The means by which the gods were propitiated, or brought on side, was the building of a shrine or idol to bow down to. Idol worship was a lever by which human beings could reduce the likelihood of something terrible happening; it was a means of ensuring a safer, better future. In the face of an endlessly uncertain world, idol worship gave human beings a means of reducing anxiety—a mechanism of control.

Idol worship gets to the heart of one of the very fundamental conditions in which we exist—time. Human beings live continually on the precipice of time. Ahead of us is a void, a dawning chasm over which we have no prescience or foresight. We face the future blind. We can look back but we cannot peel forward the pages of the future to see what is coming next.

One of the strangest human phenomena is that most of us, most of the time, do not walk around in a state of continual panic and terror. We should do! None of us know if our house will still be standing tomorrow, whether the sun will rise again, or whether our heart will beat for another minute. We make assumptions about the continuity of life simply on the basis of past experiences. The Western mind has learned to make such assumptions by extrapolating some models and laws which seem to have explanatory power for how the world has operated up to this point. We have no justification in assuming that the world will continue to operate in these ways in the future, but we choose to believe in it. This is one of our idols. This is part of our means of control.

This subordination of our minds, bodies and economies to these assumptions allows us a freedom and confidence unprecedented in the history of our species. We fly round the planet trusting our bodies to it; we lie still under the anaesthetist's mask trusting our organs to it. Because we make these assumptions we live in relative calm.

The ancients had no such scientific idol. They, instead, made use of images, totems and rituals by which they could secure their future. The instruction not to make an image of the LORD, the name of the God who had brought the people out of slavery in Egypt, is given because God defines himself uniquely as the one who will keep his word. This God is called YHWH— I am who I am, or I will be who I will be. The God who rescues his people is a God who is consistent within his own self-ascription; he is not defined or determined by that which is other than himself. As Karl Barth puts it, this same God, who is defined by the characteristic of 'love' in the New Testament, is 'the One who loves in freedom'.

This God, who will be who he will be, promises and commits himself to be for the people. He enters into a covenant with them by which he commits himself to be on their side. His refusal to tolerate an image made in his likeness is a demand that his people abandon their attempts to secure the favour of capricious and unreliable gods who cannot be trusted in themselves. Instead, He exhorts his people to trust that the LORD, the one who will be who he has chosen to be, is for them. If the LORD is for them then they do not need to fear for the future. The future has ceased to be anxious and fearful and uncertain; instead the future has been secured by the promise of God. This is the implication of the covenant.

The banishment of idolatry in the Judaeo-Christian tradition is, therefore, on the basis of the antidote that a relationship with YHWH, the LORD, offers the narrative of a fearful future. Idolatry is not primarily about images; it is about control. Redemption by the biblical God involves relinquishing control in favour of trusting that the unknown future will be secured by the faithfulness of the God who describes himself as 'for you'. This God cannot be coerced, persuaded, leveraged or 'bought' to be 'for you' through any act of sacrifice of idolatry. It is not in our power to control him. He is for you, because he chooses to be for you.

There are, then, two states in which one can inhabit the world: the first is in fear, living in an inherently unsafe world and seeking any means possible to secure a less threatening, safer future; the second is where one's future is secured only by the promise of a divine Other who offers only his word as assurance.

Therefore, the casting of the Golden Calf was a retreat into the life of fear, a life in which hostility and uncertainty are negotiated through propitiating the capricious gods. The objective guilt in that act was the wilful choice to disbelieve that God was for them, that they would be safe, in favour of a retreat into the fear narrative that the world was fundamentally unsafe. This same narrative is repeated on numerous occasions throughout the Old and New Testaments, always with the same implications. We see this when the Israelites, on the borders of the land of Canaan just weeks after leaving Egypt, send out spies. Reports come back from the spies of the size and strength of the occupiers. Despite the appeals of loyal Caleb to trust that the LORD would give the land into their hands as he has promised, the people retreat to the fear narrative. The condemnation for this is that none of that generation will be allowed to enter the land; thus they wander for forty years until they are all dead.

We see this, too, when Moses pleads with the LORD to go with the people. Moses has understood that the fundamental posture of the people of the LORD is one of presence; God is with them. It is only on this basis that they can exist. If God is no longer with them then they cannot move forward. God's presence is not merely proximity, but it is also commitment; it signifies protection, provision and communication. It is the presence of God that is the antidote to the fear narrative. And God's presence cannot be manipulated or maintained by any act of worship or sacrifice by the people. God must choose, in his freedom, to go with them. It is within the nature of this covenant relationship that the people are made safe only by trust in God. They have no agency to recruit it.

In contrast to Moses, we read how King Saul is rejected as king when he steps in to offer the sacrifice prior to a battle. The prophet Samuel has specifically instructed Saul to wait for him to arrive and offer the sacrifice before commencing the fight. Samuel, however, is late. Saul is getting anxious, because the battle must be started and God's blessing must be recruited, so he offers the sacrifice himself. At this moment, Samuel walks over the brow of the hill and declares God's rejection of Saul. Saul had retreated to the fear narrative, the one of sacrifice as an act of co-opting the presence and power of God to be for him, in order to the face the threat of war.

Chapter 2

The Fear Narrative and the Invitation to the Kingdom

"Fear is the mother of morality."

Friedrich Nietzsche

We tend to conceive of the act of following Jesus as an act of moral reform. Matthew is called away from his tax desk; Zacchaeus gives away half of his wealth and four times what he has defrauded; the man born blind is told to sin no more; the high-minded Nicodemus is humbled; the tax collector at the temple pleads, 'God have mercy on me, a sinner'; the promiscuous and lascivious prodigal returns, repentant, to a life of moderation and loyalty.

Similarly, today, we tend to depict the choice to follow Jesus as one that leads to a reform of our personal and moral standards. We expect the new convert, at least within a year or two, to change the coarse language they use, the way they treat others, what they watch with their eyes, the stories they tell in the playground, and the way they use their money. It is true that New Testament writers focus in great depth on the moral character of the life of those in the Kingdom. But moral reform only makes sense in this way when we sit within the guilt narrative that I have been explaining.

The guilt narrative conceives of the fundamental problem that exists between God and man as a judicial one. There is an impassable moral gulf which can only be bridged by the sacrificial death of Jesus himself. He, by his act of sacrifice, makes atonement for our misdeeds and changes our guilty status irremovably to that of pardoned. The guilt narrative continues that, therefore, it is only those who recognise their sin (their guilty verdict) who will plead for this pardon and thus receive it; and it is only those who have received it who will, in gratitude, seek to change their lives, living in a new way according to the law and will of God. In this narrative, moral reform is central to the move from being outside the Kingdom to being in the Kingdom—not as a means of entry (which would involve some notion of justification by works) but as a mark of entry (the subsequent out-workings of the power of the Holy Spirit in us).

How does the fear narrative alter this story, if at all? The fear narrative suggests that the fundamental fault line in the world, from Genesis chapter 3, is that the world is now no longer safe. Each of us, therefore, comes into a world in which we are under threat. Because survival is our chief concern, we therefore develop mechanisms to make ourselves safe in the world. One of the archetypal mechanisms is the developing of a front and a back stage—one version of our self that we show to the world and one that we hide away. By such means, we seek to ensure a favourable response from the watching audience. Few of us could survive the disapproval of those around us on a continual basis. Remember, the odds are not good!

The fear narrative suggests that guilt, objectively, is a social recognition that social relationships have been disrupted. Someone has been hurt in some way, and therefore seeks retribution, revenge, or reparation. Guilt alerts us to threat—there is now danger and hostility in play. We are afraid. The emotion of fear leads to all kinds of acts of hostility in return, starting with the story of Cain and Abel. However, the one of whom we are most afraid is God himself—hence the response in the Garden of Eden to hide and reveal selectively. God is now no longer reliably for us. The fear narrative suggests that such a view of God—or the gods—defines religions based on idolatry, in which different means are used to secure the favours of the capricious gods who are not reliably for you. By such means, a measure of control is asserted over the unknown future that we face, standing, as we do, on the precipice of time.

The God of the bible, the God who enters into covenant—YHWH—invites his people into a uniquely different posture with regard to him and to the world. He asserts that their future will be made secure by his promise that he will be for them. I will come to the propitiatory mechanism by which God makes this promise later in this book. The shift, though, involves the risk of relinquishing the acts that one has previously relied upon to gain some control over the future, in favour of trusting entirely on the commitment of this God to be for you.

In the New Testament, what we see is a more forensic, intimate collection of encounters with individuals and groups to whom Jesus extends the invitation to enter the Kingdom. The response to this invitation is fundamentally one of risk. The key choice individuals are invited to make involves giving up that which has made them secure in favour of trusting that Jesus himself will secure them. What characterises entry into the Kingdom, therefore, is not moral reform but risk. Are those individuals willing to risk letting go of what they have used to secure them and trust that they will be secured by Jesus? Are we?

If we look again, we see this narrative of risk at the heart of almost all the encounters Jesus has with people. Zacchaeus must risk losing his financial security to enter the Kingdom; Nicodemus, his intellectual credibility; the Centurion, his authority; the fishermen, their livelihoods; even the disabled man sitting by the water waiting to be stirred must choose whether he really wants to give up the familiarity and safety of his life by the pool in order to be healed. In fact, Jesus goes on to teach that discipleship fundamentally involves risk and exposure: one must leave father and mother, brother and sister. Foxes have holes and birds have nests but the son of man has no place to lay his head. The life of discipleship is fundamentally one of risk, one of relinquishing familiar habits and relying instead upon God's provision.

The groups of people who seem least able to hear and receive the invitation are those who cling on to their structures of life. The teachers of the law, with their formal social codes that give them status and financial security, are unable to embrace the radical provision of the Kingdom. The citizens of Nazareth, Jesus' hometown, are unable to reform their social perspective about Jesus. Isn't this the carpenter, Joseph's son? They choose to hold onto the familiar ways in which they see and live in their world, rejecting the prophet in their midst. So it is with the rich, morally upright, young man who comes to Jesus enquiring how to gain eternal life. To him, Jesus offers devastating words: 'Go, sell everything you have, give to the poor and then come and follow me.' This is a story we shall look at in greater depth a little later, but for now let us just note that this call to give up all he had is not a call for all Christians to live in poverty, but rather for this young fellow to relinquish his existing means of security.

Luke situates this encounter between two other dialogues in order to sharpen and highlight the point he wants to make. The story is introduced to us through the event of the little children crowding around Jesus. The disciples want to send them away, for they are a distraction and an irritation slowing proceedings up. Jesus, on the other hand, welcomes them in his arms and teaches us that the Kingdom belongs to such as these.

Belongs to such as these? To children? To those who have no knowledge or understanding? To those who have made no formal choice or commitment to follow? How absurd! How ludicrous! Yes, says Jesus, the Kingdom belongs to such as these. And just at that moment, the young man arrives. There could be no greater contrast between the two: children come to us, dependent, trusting the goodwill of their parents. They get into our cars at the beginning of a journey with no notion where they are going or how they will be fed; yet they are not fearful, not worriedly stoking up with bread before they leave in case there is no food provided. The children live trusting that their father and mother are good and will provide for their needs. By contrast, this young man—moral, upright, well respected—has no need to trust anyone. He has at his disposal the education, finances and respect to negotiate all that life may throw at him.

Let the little children come to me, says Jesus, for to such belongs the Kingdom of God. And then he tells the man to go and sell all he has and to follow him, for in this way he will live in the Kingdom.

The man goes away sad, for he has great wealth. How hard it is for the rich to enter the Kingdom of heaven! How confused the disciples are! How radically Jesus is overturning their notions of the Kingdom. For the Kingdom is fundamentally characterised not by moral goodness, piety or devotion, but by risk—the willingness to abandon that with which we have tried to make ourselves secure, whether this is money, skills, status, privilege or relationships, in favour of trusting that God himself will secure our future. This is the move from paganism to Christianity. This is the singular shift from a posture of fear in the world to a posture of being made safe by God.

The Absurdity of the Gospel

What becomes clear, as we read the Gospel stories is that the invitation Jesus is making is no soft option. Discipleship is not some behavioural modification; it is not even radical piety; it is not, even, as we will discover later through Paul, giving up one's life to the cause in death. It involves something far less certain, far more ludicrous. It involve abandoning every shred of security we had stitched around ourselves to make ourselves safe in an unsafe world in favour of trusting singularly in a God to make us safe.

The archetypal story that illustrates this act of faith is that of Peter being invited to walk towards Jesus on water. Peter and the other disciples are rowing their way across the lake at night when Jesus comes to them, walking on the surface of the water. Peter, once he has confirmed who it is, asks Jesus to call him out to him. Come, says Jesus. Come—the invitation Jesus makes to all to follow him. Come, leave the life you have been inhabiting, leave the place of work, or pattern you have been stitching together for yourself. Come.

So Peter comes. And as he fixes his eyes on Jesus, his feet do not sink beneath the water's surface. Peter is held up, despite the fact that he has abandoned all physical means to hold himself up. He is outside the boat; he has relinquished control. He is ludicrously insecure. And yet, he is deeply safe. He is held by his gaze to the one who has committed himself to Peter's well being.

The disciples had been rowing hard against the wind, struggling to move themselves forward. Jesus does not come and offer to row with them. He does not come and take over. He does not invest their arms with extra strength. He does not suggest they turn back. He does not encourage them to row with the wind; nor does he change the direction of the wind. Instead, he invites Peter to get out of the boat. Discipleship involves abandoning all mechanisms by which we have been coping, getting by, making ourselves safe, in favour of trusting the invitation of God, expressed directly to Peter, to be made safe in him.

Repentance and Faith

Now this story is not an invitation for all followers of Jesus to jump off the next boat they find themselves in and prove God's provision for them. Nor is it an invitation to stop, in a reckless fashion, doing the things that make our lives work. There is a specificity here which we should not read ourselves into. However, we should place ourselves within the narrative of a God whose invitation to us is to be made safe singularly through his attention on us.

This is the point of coherence with the other stories in the Gospels where individuals choose to abandon their strategies in favour of trusting in Jesus to be for them. This is also the insight into the nature of repentance and faith. Repentance is not to be seen centrally as a moral change, a turning away from wrong things. Rather, it is to be understood as an abandonment of all the strategies we have deployed to secure ourselves outside a relationship with a divine Father.

The Relationship of Fear and Guilt

I have been suggesting that fear, rather than guilt, is the primal fault line that describes the sinful condition. However, I am not saying that there is no such thing as guilt. Nor am I downplaying guilt, suggesting that the human condition is not as bad as a 'guilt narrative' might suggest. Nor am I suggesting that guilt is a negative emotion that we should reject. Rather, I am proposing that guilt, as an objective status, is a derivative of the objective status of hostility. Attempts to make ourselves safe in the world outside a trusting relationship with our divine father leads to spirals of fear and hostility towards others—acts of aggression, defiance, territoriality, concealment, invasion, denial and so on.

Such acts further disrupt the objective safety in the world, breaking trust, fostering anger and encouraging the desire for retribution. As we are acted upon, so we act in fear. Out of fear we try to coordinate a world in which we are in control; damage to us is mitigated and our physical, emotional and social needs are met. Such acts often necessitate 'using' other people as commodities for our own ends, colluding with people for mutual gain, withdrawing from or attacking people who are a threat. Every such act is an act of guilt. We are objectively guilty for we have responsibility for it. We do not have to behave that way, but we often choose to. We therefore shoulder our responsibility.

However, we are not the only ones responsible. There is a causal chain, a nexus of fear, in which we find ourselves living. A wider community, past and present, is complicit in my guilt. Guilt also lies elsewhere. I am victim as well as perpetrator. Guilt, therefore, describes the outcomes of my actions to preserve myself, whilst fear describes the cause. Guilt looks at the out-workings of a fallen world, whilst fear describes the root energy, the primal fault line. The two narratives do not compete with each other, but rather interpret each other. Guilt relates to fear as the heat of an oven relates to the flow of gas which burns inside it.

The Fear of the Lord

I have been suggesting that the central fault line in the human condition is the breach of trust, from which the world, and primarily God, is experienced no longer as safe but unsafe. The Gospel, then, fundamentally resolves this posture of fear by removing the hostility of God as threat. However, there are numerous references throughout the scriptures to the beneficial value of 'the fear of the Lord'.

We are told that 'The fear of the Lord is the beginning of wisdom'. It is important to understand the proper and toxic fear of God which I have been describing. Paul encourages Timothy by reminding him that, in Christ, he did not receive a spirit, which makes him a slave again to fear. Rather, he received a spirit of power, love and self-discipline. This power, love and self-discipline is very like the wisdom which we have been told the 'fear of the Lord' will engender in us. Wisdom is not mere knowledge but rather a commitment to a right posture in life. In relation to the Lord, therefore, this kind of fear is understood as a kind of appropriate recognition. To 'fear' God is to understand, in one's living, that God is the source of power and authority in the world. Therefore, he is the one around which we ought to orientate our lives, rather than some rival.

As the old hymn has it: 'Fear him you saints and you will then have nothing else to fear' (based on Psalm 34.9). Fear of the Lord is the subordination of our own agency, as well as our recruiting of other agencies, to make ourselves safe in the world. The fear the Lord is to seek no other source of safety other than him.

Chapter 3

The Architecture of Sin and the Relationship with the Self

"I was a personality before I became a person. I am simple, complex, generous, selfish, unattractive, beautiful, lazy and driven."

Barbara Streisand

To understand the centrality of the distinction I am making between repentance as risk rather than moral reform, we need to think a little more deeply about the nature of guilt and of sin. We often think of 'sin' as something outside of and distinct from 'us'. We sometimes use the language of sin as stain: we, an unblemished object, have become tainted and stained by sin. Or we think of sin as the bad habits we have got into which we must choose to break. Or we think of sin as the things and actions we do wrong, separate from 'us', our being, making the distinction that 'God hates the sin but loves the sinner'.

The model underlying all of these images of sin is rather like a fried egg. The identity—the 'I'—is the yolk in the centre. This 'I' is what God created, what he intended, and what he is redeeming. It is this 'I' that he will preserve beyond death—the real us, the essence. However, around the 'I' has gathered a host of 'bad stuff', represented by the white of the egg. We are surrounded by it; it has got attached to us; and we carry it around.

In this model, we can observe God as a kind of divine chef, slicing away with his knife at the white of sin that clings to us, paring us back to the real essence he created us to be. We use the language of 'finding our true identity in Christ' or 'rediscovering who we were meant to be in Christ'. We talk about God 'restoring his image in us'. This model preserves the 'I' from the acts of sinning that happen on the periphery. It relies on a distinction between doing and being, and suggests that what we do is not actually part of who we are.

The guilt narrative lends weight to this depiction of sin and its relationship with our identity. We are guilty of things we have done wrong, which need to be punished, cleaned away and then not returned to. The Gospel is the washer's powder, able to cleanse the filthy rags and remake them (us) sparkling and white. Guilt evokes images of dirt, blackness and filth, as opposed to innocence, which, in our iconography, we conceive of as white and shining.

Sin, however, properly understood in the fear narrative, is all of our attempts to make ourselves safe in an unsafe world. It is a posture that says 'I am on my own; I must recruit sufficient resources around myself to cope'. Sin as a coping strategy creates a problem for the dissection of 'me' and the 'act of sin'. The problem lies in the fact that much of what I have come to call 'me' can be forensically identified as a central and integral part of that coping strategy. In other words, my sin and I are coterminous, one and the same.

Let me explain this in the following way. Imagine that you met me. One of the things you may say after talking to me is that 'Simon is a thoughtful and articulate person' (possibly, or possibly not...). Over time, if a friendship grew between us, you may gain the confidence to say something fuller, such as 'Simon—well he's got a thoughtful nature; he's reasonably intelligent and likes to have clear reasons for what he believes. He's a thinker and a reflector before a doer'.

Imagine that I then completed a personality test, for example. In it I am asked a series of questions about whether I tend first to think rather than speak, how I approach problems, how much I like to read rather than watch films, whether I like to have reasons for my beliefs, whether I tend to argue for my opinions if others disagree with me, and so on. At the end of this personality test I am provided with a report which offers me a narrative about my personality. Amongst many other things, it says: 'Simon is a thoughtful, carefully reasoned person who likes to know why he believes what he does. He will rarely be rushed into a decision and will often choose to argue his case if he feels he needs to'. I show this report to you and you respond: 'Simon, I'm not at all surprised. We always knew you were like this.'

A couple of weeks later, you hear from another friend that I have upset them by having a disagreement with them. You sympathise. 'That's typical Simon, isn't it? It's because he's such a thinker that he always has to challenge other people's ideas when he thinks they are wrong.' Later that day, you phone me up and, during the conversation, say: 'Simon, that argument you had with Tom left him a bit upset, you know. We know you always need people to be consistent in their ideas. That's just you. As a thinker, you can't change that, and it's a gift actually. But sometimes you aren't aware of how that affects other people. Maybe next time try to be a little more sensitive to the impact you have on others who are different from you?'

I go away from this discussion conscious of two things; first, I am a 'thinker', and, second, I need to be careful because as a thinker I can upset others who are different from me.

This narrative of self, I suggest, is probably one that most of us can relate to. In fact, I would suggest that in the West it is the universal norm for how we think about self, identity, actions, gifts and talents. Underneath, we have a notion that there is an 'I' and that this 'I' has certain fixed characteristics. In this case, one of those is that 'I' am a 'thinker'. I cannot change this 'I'; it is part of me. A test may diagnose my personality as a thinking one. This is just something that I was born with. In some ways it is in my genes. Those who do not like it may choose not to be my friend, and those who do stay in touch with me. As I have grown up, I may have become more aware of the characteristics of my 'I' than I was as a young man, and this enables me to be more careful and sensitive about the self I share with others. I cannot change myself but I can understand that not all people are like me. I can learn how to bring my 'I' into the party without crushing or dominating the 'I' of others.

In the narrative of guilt and the fried egg, this all fits very neatly. 'I' am the yolk: I cannot change that, for it is me, my essence; it is who God made me to be. I need to celebrate that. Unfortunately, 'I' sometimes behave in a way that diminishes life for others—through carelessness, thoughtlessness, dominance, attention seeking, etc. This is 'sin'; this is the white around the yolk of 'I'. This is the selfish behaviour that God is in the business of carving away through the process of sanctification. One day, though not this side of heaven, I will be fully 'prepared'—or perhaps better 'pared'—for heaven, and 'I', the pure, restored yolk, freed of my surrounding mantle of sin, will be fit to enter heaven and enjoy full coherent community with other saints.

But let us look at this story again, because there are some things in it which do not, in fact, work. First of all, the neat division between the yolk of 'I' and the bad acts of the surrounding white is not actually true. Travel back into my past with me. My father was a scientist and, as it happened, taught at my secondary school. I have half of his genes in me and, whilst as a young boy I showed no great aptitude for science, I found that logical reasoning started to click with me around the age of thirteen. I started to score well in the sciences. It felt good to come high up the class order in a subject and so I would put extra effort into my science homework. My father was a great sounding board and our increasingly long scientific discussions in the evenings helped me improve my thinking and get good grades, and they also forged a father-son bond between us at a critical age.

Science, rational thought, and empirical evidence became my currency; I could trade it for affection and attention from my father and credibility at school. In a dangerous world of teenage boarding-school life, rational thought became a weapon for me and I deployed it as much as I could. I duly achieved top grades, was awarded prizes, and entered Oxford. By now, if you had met me, I would have told you that I was a scientist and a strong thinker. Studying Biology at Oxford—a university that believes in the benefits of intellectual neglect to foster initiative and resilience—I refined my self-concept as 'thinker'. By then a committed Christian, I used my mind to develop rigorous apologetic arguments for the truth of the Gospel. My friends and fellow students knew me as having a strong, rational faith and clear convictions. It gave me confidence in myself to win arguments about faith and science, the divinity of Christ and the evidence for the resurrection. The skills and aptitudes that I had cultivated for rigorous argument combined with my intolerance of sloppy thinking provided meaning and reason in response to the chaos of the world. Clear-minded planning gave me an effective approach to my life; it was my weapon. But it was also me.

Perhaps you can see how it would have been impossible to separate these two. There was the 'I' who you met as a friend and who was mirrored back to me in a personality test. There was also the 'me' who sequestered an intellectual asset to survive school and build a sense of self-confidence as a young adult in the world. Who I had become was a result of years of strategic behaviour, cultivating some aspects of my mind whilst neglecting others, developing a certain vocabulary (and with it, accent, posture, style and rhetoric) and eschewing others. My identity, as a twenty-something-year-old adult, was the result of my acts to defend myself in the world. It was my means of ensuring that I received sufficient attention, praise, affirmation, status and power. It gave me assurance about who I was and a position in the world. It was whom you had come to see me as and whom you expected to meet if we chanced to bump into each other in the pub.

Now, this is not to say that all of my 'thinking skill' was merely a Machiavellian attempt to dominate my world and ward off all hostile threats. Nor is it to say that my thinking has no genetic seeds within it. But it is to say that the formation of the person you now call Simon Walker, and who I label to myself as 'me', cannot be disentangled from the strategies that a growing boy cultivated to cope with the world he found himself in.

I have illustrated this in relation to one simple aspect of me—my ability to think. I could equally do so for other aspects of me such as my attitude to risks, confidence in groups, willingness to concede, ability to empathise, toleration of stress, tendency to be anxious, and, indeed, all aspects of my 'personality'. In fact, if I had to offer an overall account of my personality, I would have to say that it is my embedded strategy that I have come to iterate habitually over time. It is a strategy which involves my thinking, speaking, acting and feeling in the world. This strategy has become so familiar to me that I now refer to it as my 'personality'.

This narrative of self challenges the 'fried egg' model of self and sin. It asserts that, neat though the model is, it simply is not possible to tease apart the 'I' of the yolk from the white of my actions (sinful or otherwise). My actions and I are tied up together; I am the product of the story I have lived and the strategies I have deployed. In fact, it is not actually possible to talk about 'me' as a finished, self-contained self at all. 'I', as an entity in the world, am not yet finished. I am open, uncontained, and still in the process of coming into being.

More than that, 'I' am a messy mixture of good and bad. The person I have become is a result of choices I have made, behaviours I have cultivated, and skills I have nursed and tended which have made me safe in an unsafe world. I, and my strategies to cope with being in an unsafe world, are all bound up together. Those strategies have been shaped by emotions of fear, the need for control, the desire for prestige and the longing for relationships. At times, I have used others for my own ends; at times, I have been curt, hostile or dominating. At times I have been greedy, impatient and acquisitive. At times I have been fearful, depressive and recalcitrant. At other times I have been charming, warm and personable.

I am, in fact, much less like a fried egg, and much more like a ball of wool that has been knitted into a particular, unique shape. Its pattern, though discernible and in some ways beautiful, is also full of knots and ties where the wool has caught and snagged. The knitted form, still unfinished, takes its structure from all of the snags and catches along the way. These are not simply unintended mistakes; they also represent the intentional, committed ways I have threaded my needle to dominate other people, avoid being hurt, reassure myself of my worth and recruit praise. Even the best, finest bits of my knitted self are an attempt to coordinate other people's knitting around me in order to feel whole and strong and held.

The identity of 'my sin' and the identity of 'me' are intertwined. I cannot tease them apart. If we employ psychological language, we find ourselves having to acknowledge that the way we have come to feel, think, judge, act, love, fear, get angry and be morose is, to some extent, an outworking of our attempts to make ourselves safe in this fundamentally unsafe world. My sin is stitched into my psychological texture.

Let me give you another personal example, one I referred to in the book's Introduction. I used to think that my depression was an illness. I spent most of a decade, in my twenties, cycling into increasingly deep depressions until I finally collapsed into what one might call a breakdown. I remember feeling tremendous relief in my GP's medical diagnosis that I was depressed and needed some drug treatment. It was, for me, so important at the time to be able to label my depression as an illness. It was something I could do nothing about—a chemical imbalance, a serotonin deficit, a result of my genetic make-up running in the family. My depression was something I would have to learn to live with and adapt to. I would probably live on a low level of anti-depressants all my life.

It was only after a number of years that I began to examine this story again and see that, neat though it was, it was not actually true. My depression was, in the main, a result of patterns of thought and behaviour, which I had come to cultivate over a number of years as an adolescent and young adult. Finding myself in a high-performing university, involved in a Christian ministry which fast-tracked students into leadership through mentoring schemes, I had learned how to secure powerful affirmation from those around me. To use the metaphor of my front and back stage, I learned how to deliver a performance in the Simon Walker theatre to the audience of highly vocal critics whose good opinions I could not risk losing, and how to achieve standing ovations. However, producing such performances night after night, year after year, was proving to be unsustainable.

What started to happen was that I would move on, after two or three years. Without realising it, what I was doing was putting a sign on the theatre door announcing: 'Show Stopped–Reopening in X'. Then I would start again, elsewhere, where the critics were not expecting so much of the show, at least to start with. However, the strategy did not work because my own psychological formation had left me expecting the critics to be picky and negative about the slightest failures. Soon, therefore, I had to work just as hard to avoid their negative reports on the new show, and each performance was a fearful avoidance of their rejection of me and of falling short of the unreasonably high standards I had set myself.

My depression, increasingly, became the mechanism by which I could legitimately put a 'Show Stopped' notice on the theatre door. No one could criticise you if you were ill, not even yourself. No one could expect anything of you if you were depressed. Depression–although it was a black, hulking, enervating, hole into which I would crawl and from which I would see nothing as of any worth–was at least safe. In that place I could not be rejected. In that place I did not risk the disapproval of the significant critics in my audience who held the keys, in my mind, to life and death.

It was a shock for me to realise that, whilst of course there was a chemical story to my depression (for I was prone to it and probably still do have genetically low serotonin levels), I had learned to depend on this strategy to cope in the world. For me, as for many depressives, the choice NOT to be depressed was the hardest one in the world.

Choosing not to be depressed involved choosing to reject this myth that performances in my 'theatre' always had to have amazing reviews. It involved choosing to let people see the show broken down, with the signs hanging off the door, and the actor sitting on the stage saying, 'Well, this is just it—this is me'. It involved letting people into my messy, fragile, complex, confused, doubting, dark back stage, and not just my front stage. It involved choosing to trust people and to trust myself to people. In short, it involved choosing to be undefended. It involved choosing life.

My identity and my sin were coordinated together. You could not, and cannot, tease them apart. I am the messy, intertwining knots of wool being stitched together into a partial, frayed, unfinished pattern. The Gospel, I came to realise, was not God's forgiveness of the bad stuff and then the slicing away of the white around the good yolk. The Gospel went deeper. The Gospel was not about paring away the sin in order to get back to real me. It was about re-stitching my whole story from start to finish. I realised that I needed to allow God's love to penetrate my story far more systemically and far more fundamentally. This Gospel would set me free and, in the process, 'who I was' would fundamentally change.

Everything I was and everything I had was up for grabs. All my strategies, skills, assets, behaviours—good and bad—through which I had forged my career, all of them had to be available for God to re-knit into a new coordinated pattern. Sanctification was an infinitely more penetrating, dissembling and de-structuring process than I had ever conceived of before. Sanctification was to involve the very threads of my life being unpicked and re-stitched in a new form, a form woven in freedom rather than fear.

The Strategies of Sin

Sin is a myriad of varied strategies, woven by us, intimately part of us, the very threads of our lives, intertwined with our histories—the fabric of how we have come to secure ourselves in this hostile and uncertain world. Some people cope by retreating, hiding themselves away on their back stage and giving little of themselves to others. Others cope by projecting a persona of confidence and dominance around them, and in so doing they may trample on the fragile selves of others.

Some people collude with those in power, finding their safety through alliances, and they are never able to say no. Others seek safety in the crowd, sensing the moods around them, tuning in, and working out how to stay in with the group. Others define themselves against the group, reassuring themselves of their own individuality and identity through their postures of resistance and autonomy. Others recruit symbols, trappings and artefacts to project their importance in society, feeding off the adulation and power. Others maintain rigid control in their lives, ordering events in such a way that they are never caught out. Others contain their vulnerabilities—their fears, feelings and real thoughts—never risking letting them be examined, exposed, shared or helped by another, and never trusting another to make themselves safe.

Some live by orthodoxies, formulas and doctrines that define who is right and who is wrong, who is in and who is out, who is safe and who is a threat. Others run away from threat by living only with the broken, soothing the needy and tending their own emotional deficits through the shared pain of another's wounded life.

And to this, Jesus comes and calls us to be free. Jesus comes and calls us to repent. He calls us to abandon the fears that hold us and to relinquish control of the behaviours and habits, the norms and ideas, the attitudes and beliefs that we have laboriously coordinated as a means of surviving. He comes to set us free—free from fear, free from the suffocating, dying traps we have snared ourselves in.

Thus the Gospel is, for each one of us, different. Jesus' invitation to us is no singular, general call to repent and believe. It is a unique and specific word to me to repent—to give up, turn from and abandon the particular strategies I have been adopting in favour of being made safe in relationship with him.

Chapter 4

Narratives of Redemption and the Centrality of Trust

"Being deeply loved by someone gives you strength,

while loving someone deeply gives you courage."

Lao Tse

The key ingredient that has determined our experience of the world as unsafe is that of trust—broken trust. Adam and Eve chose not to trust that God was for them. As trust broke, the future became uncertain and unsafe. Their, and our, behaviours from that point became the means of anticipating and avoiding potential threats to secure a favourable response from a potentially threatening audience. Therefore, if the Gospel is to have redemptive power over the human condition, the Gospel must centrally address the issue of trust. It must have the power to reverse our experience of broken trust and bring us to a reality in which we can fundamentally trust again. This transition must be sufficient to ensure that we can inhabit the world as safe—safe at its core—and therefore one in which we do not have to behave out of fear. Unless the Gospel can restore trust in relationships then it is powerless to redeem the fallen condition of the world.

However, trust is not a general, conceptual reality. Trust comes from the knowledge of a particular individual. It is specific to a relationship between one person and another. When trust breaks down so, too, does the relationship erode. And the nature of our experience of trust is often related to the relationships we experienced as children with our parents and our surrogate parent figures.

The experiences of trust we have as children remain imprinted on us throughout the rest of our lives. A child gets into a car with her parents and trusts that she will be safe, that she will be fed and brought to a bed that night. The future for her is not anxious because she knows from experience those who have the power to secure her future. She trusts them.

John Bowlby, the father and architect of attachment theory, refers to the 'working models' we form as children, which continue to guide our predictions of whether people will be trustworthy. Neuropsychologically, we understand better than ever before that our emotional memories are not easily eroded over time. The experiences of our early years have a profound and lasting influence on our adult selves. Positive and negative experiences shape that which we become.

To deploy a metaphor, the colour of the wool that we weave in our early years remains the dominant and persistent hue throughout the fabric our lives. Weave in red, and the basic, overall hue of the garment will continue to be warm tones. Weave in blue, and it will remain blue. Weave in green and it will be green.

Rather like the four primary colours, there appear to be four primary hues of 'trust' that people stitch their lives from. The first (let us call it green) is woven from low trust of others and low trust of oneself. The second (let us call it yellow) is stitched from high trust of others but low trust of oneself. The third (let us call it blue) is stitched from low trust of others but high trust of oneself. And the fourth (let us call it red) is stitched from high trust of others and high trust of self. These four different hues relate to widely acknowledged models of attachment. They also relate to the four different ego patterns that I have depicted in my former books on undefended leadership.

	Trust of others	
Trust of self	GREEN HUED SELF Low trust of others Low trust of oneself	YELLOW HUED SELF High trust of others Low trust of oneself
	BLUE HUED SELF Low trust of others High trust of oneself	RED HUED SELF High trust of others High trust of oneself

Chart 1. Showing four ego patterns (from Leading Out of Who You Are, Simon P Walker, 2007)

4.1 The Green Hued Self

Low trust of others; low trust of oneself

The lack of trustworthy relationships early in life can leave some children endlessly suspicious of future relationships. More than that, they may also lose trust in themselves as individuals. Trusting oneself appropriately means having a sense of self-worth and an appropriate sense of boundaries. We are not beholden only to the wishes and demands of others; we can influence events around us. To lose trust in oneself is to feel powerless to change events and thus vulnerable to the impact of others. To lack trust in both oneself and others is to face a world which is almost endlessly unsafe.

The upshot of this, in the long run, is a person with a sustained sense of suspicion; betrayals are 'seen' all around them, slights perceived when they were not intended, and disloyalties punished with instant withdrawal. This person has cultivated an acute awareness of the motives, intents and moods of others; for this person life involves fearfully avoiding being hurt. They use their acuity to negotiate relationships and monitor the surrounding conditions, propitious or otherwise.

When they come to God, they anticipate a divinity that will, at best, be unreliable, like human relationships are for them. They will both long for a 'resting place' of a secure and safe relationship and also fear the level of commitment involved in attaining it. The risk may not be worth the reward. Perhaps better a God who is held at arm's length rather than risking being let down, as has happened so often in the past.

The redemption of such a person cannot involve some mere statement of God's love for us. Nor does this person need to be told, crushingly, of their guilt and unworthiness. These messages persistently resonate loud and clear in their heads; they know them well. For them, the effects of the sin of others have woven the threads of their fears. For them the Gospel, if it is to be good news at all, must offer them dignity and security; the gospel must be a promise of reliability and consistent intimacy. In and through the Gospel this person must come to know not only God as trustworthy but themselves as worthy of trust. If they are to abandon their coping strategies to embrace an open and undefended way of living, the master craftsman must re-stitch the garment of their identity. He must replace the hues of fear and mistrust of self and others with a thread of a different hue, one that allows the freedom to trust.

The woman who could trust nobody, not even herself

There was once a woman who trusted neither herself nor other people. She had not always been so untrusting. In fact, she used to be a warm and open person, always believing in the best in people. But something happened that changed all that. She got into a relationship with a man who turned out to be a bully. Little by little he crushed her self-confidence and then, when she no longer held any value for him, he threw her out. Despite the man's behaviour, she was the one people scorned and shamed as if she was the cause of the breakdown.

She lived in a country where there was no social security and no provision for single women. So, she was thrown back onto her few remaining assets—her beauty was one of them. Exploiting her charms, she got herself another man, an older man this time, someone she hoped would prove to be kinder. He was, and, for a while, she was happy. It seemed as if her difficult past was behind her. But tragedy struck and he contracted a degenerative disease. She nursed him in his remaining months but he was dead within the year.

Little was known about such medical conditions in the society in which she lived. The people believed that, in some way, she was the cause of the illness and that she was in some way cursed—or at least that she brought ill fate to those who knew her. After that, life became more and more impossible. It was like a terrible, vicious spiral, getting worse all the time. She fell in and out of relationship and relationship— she used men as a means of providing her with some protection and intimacy and men used her for cheap sex. She loathed herself for what she had been brought down to. She found that when she walked down the street other women would cross over to avoid her or spit at her feet, disgusted by her immoral behaviour.

Of course, she used to bluff, as if this was water off a duck's back. She would sneer at those little women, look down her nose, swinging her hips, burning up inside, crying inside, pleading, 'Please, please make it stop!' It got so bad that she took to avoiding contact with people altogether, even walking miles out of her way to be on her own. It was on one such daily trek that she found herself meeting a most unusual man.

She was at the well—not the one the townsfolk used in the market square, but a travellers' well, some mile or so outside the walls. This man, Jewish and in his thirties, arrives at the well. He is obviously passing through. She thinks nothing of it, ignoring his presence and keeping her eyes down, when he addresses her: 'Will you give me a drink?', he asks. She is taken aback: why is he talking to her? What does he want? Most men only want one thing, in her experience. Is this the latest chat-up line she's going to have to endure? So she bats it back: 'What are you talking to me for? You're a Jew aren't you? Yes, thought so. Well, it's obvious I'm a Samaritan. It's not a great idea you know to be "asking me for a drink", if that's really what you mean...'

Then they have a bizarre conversation. He starts talking about living water—not the stuff from the well, but some kind of spiritual water from the well inside of you...something that does not run out... something that keeps you fresh. But she is suspicious. She has heard about the Messiah idea—some guy God is going to send to bring revival, to bring people back to faith. In a funny way, she has believed that it could happen some day. She certainly wants it to happen. In truth, she would welcome anything that could change her life. God, she is tired, worn out. Parched, in fact. That idea of water from the inside sounds great.

But she has heard this before. How many men have offered her 'water'?! And how many of those promises have turned out to be empty? She should never have trusted any of them. She should never have been so gullible. The only thing she got in return was dirt kicked in her face time and again. And yet...and yet...

How odd that this guy asks her to do something for him. Most of the time, guys treated her like she was a doll or another kind of object. But she could not make them stay. They always left, leaving her with nothing, and leaving her feeling like nothing.

But this guy seems different. The way he talks to her, the look in his eyes, the fact that he believes she could do something for him. It all makes her feel, feel...well, worth something, like she matters.

It is a great feeling. But then her stomach turns as she remembers that this is a stranger. The only reason for his kindness is that he does not know her. If he knew even part of the story, his lip would curl just like the rest. So, imagine her horror then when this man asks her directly to go and get her husband. She freezes. What can she say? How can she be honest? Time slows and she feels her pulse pounding in her head. She has to choose. She hangs her head in shame: 'I don't have a husband.'

'I know that', the man replies. 'I know, in fact, that you have had five husbands and that the man you're with now is not your husband.'

It is like a bomb going off. It is not that he knows these details, although that he does is just weird. It is that he knew them and that he stayed. He knew who she was, and he still talked to her. He still looked her in the eye. He still asked her to serve him water. He still valued her.

But alongside the wonder that was beginning to well up within her came the old questions and doubts. Did he really see something good in her? And what about this message about water? Was she hearing what she wanted to hear? Was he was offering her some security, some commitment, some kind of permanent relationship? Was this man telling her that she could trust him? She had heard people talk about the Messiah. Was this what that idea was all about?

This woman's life had been one of isolation, ostracism and humiliation. Her main aim was to survive. Her appearance and postures were her only defences—a bluff to keep at bay the stares of disdain from her neighbours. The narrative of fear in her life reinforced the beliefs that she was alone and that this was all she deserved. This fear also blinded her to the possibility that it could be better, that there might be more for her. All she was fit for, she thought, was to let people use her and, if she could, to use them until they let her down.

For her, then, the Gospel was not some abstract concept of forgiveness and atonement. The Gospel, her encounter with Jesus, was one simple, single thing—safety. It is an offer to be known, committed to, understood, accepted, valued and trusted. It is a message that says, 'Be free from the life of fear and live a life of confidence in yourself and in Me'. Eternal life begins then—not in the future, but now, in the present. This Gospel offers a new means of living in the world now. It will fundamentally change the possibilities for how she lives and engages with those around her. Truly, she will be transformed.

4.2 The Yellow Hued Self

High trust of others, low trust of self

Some people grow up in relationships that are emotionally fragile. Perhaps those who care for them are emotionally unavailable or emotionally inexpressive. Perhaps they are working through unresolved emotions of their own, like depression or anger. What might the 'working models' be that children develop to secure attachment in these situations? How might these models iterate over time?

Those with emotionally unavailable or inexpressive parents may become attention seeking. How can they keep the person on the last row of the theatre from losing interest or falling asleep? Or, the child may find ways to please or serve—maybe there is particular show, song or intermission snack that this parent likes? All of these are attempts to meet the needs of the adult in order for the child to be valued and needed, to avoid being rejected.

Those whose parents have unresolved emotional issues may find their parents to be like beakers: it may be dangerous to add more to them; the feelings can overflow, leaking out in an aggressive, dangerous way. These children will often do all they can to avoid their parents' feelings erupting. They contain their own feelings because their parents have no room to look after them. What is more, some children may find ways to contain their parents' feelings as well. How do I keep mum from getting sad? How do I keep dad from getting angry?

When fundamental relationships are experienced and perceived as fragile children tend to develop a low trust of themselves but, paradoxically, a high trust of others. It is not difficult to understand the former. Neglected, they may simply lack emotional confidence. They may get into the habit of deferring their feelings and needs to those of their parent. Thus, over time, they fail to appreciate that their needs should be met. Not only so, difficult feelings they do have, like anger, cannot always be expressed for fear of breaking the relationship.

But what do they do with their anger? Often they blame themselves: 'It was my fault that I got hurt, or left out, or that my parents rowed or split up'. In this way, they can absolve their parents of blame and responsibility for what has gone on. In this way their angry feelings are resolved (and this is why they have a high trust of others: they over-trust other people). The cost is that they have had to take the blame onto themselves. They have become the guilty one. Repeatedly, over the years, this will lead to a crushing of the spirit, a breaking of self-worth, a sense of guilt and worthlessness.

At its extreme, this kind of pattern can lead to issues of self-harm and also to syndromes where people, often women, allow themselves to be mistreated and abused. They have come to see themselves as not being worthy of care or attention. They have to earn it. Indeed, the fabric of their self-identity which they have been stitching together over the years is knitted in the wool of abuse. This is who they know themselves to be. Rejecting it in favour of being treated with dignity and respect is almost impossible. Instead, they will repeatedly choose to find relationships in which their familiar story can be reiterated.

On a more subtle and probably more common level, many people live with a diminished sense of their worth. Many are over-conscientious, tending to work too hard and blaming themselves when things go wrong rather than risking conflict with other people. We know them as kind, considerate and selfless. But their conscientiousness comes at a cost to themselves and also with a hook to it. Consciously or not, their aims are to secure the affirmation they so desperately need and to prevent the rejection they so terribly fear.

If the Gospel is to be good news at all for such a person, then it must have the power to break this self-verdict. It must affirm their dignity and crown them with worth. Repentance, for them, is not to cry, 'Woe is me a sinner', for they already cry this endlessly in their heart. No, repentance for this person is to have the courage to turn away from this cry and to whisper to themselves and to others, 'I am worth something'. They can so turn on the basis that the God who made them is now for them. He trusts them and loves them. That is the verdict that matters. That is the verdict that transforms them and allows them legitimately to trust and love themselves.

The woman who trusted everyone but herself

There was once another woman who could trust other people but could not trust herself. She had a life-changing encounter with a young Jewish man, too, like the women of the well. It was a busy market day and the crowds were heaving, much worse than usual. She knew why: a man named Jesus was in town, a good man, a holy man. She had heard about him for stories had gone before him from town to town. She had heard how he had been kind to the poor and disabled. Apparently, he had even healed some of them. And he was coming to her town today. She had thought it through and decided that she was not going to miss this opportunity. She was going to try and get close to this Jesus. Not that it was going to be easy for there were so many people about and she found every kind of social occasion excruciating.

Jesus had just been approached by the ruler of the Synagogue, a man called Jairus who begged him to come to his house as his daughter was sick and dying. As Jesus went with him he was touched by this woman. Now, many people touched Jesus in that town centre: he was being jostled by everyone as his disciples pointed out; but Jesus knew this was a special touch, that power had gone out of him.

In fact, the woman had not actually touched Jesus himself, but just the hem of his robe. She had managed to slip unseen into the crowd, between the legs of the bystanders, to reach out and brush the tassels of his robe as he walked by. A single, brief act that she hoped would be unnoticed and overlooked; an act deliberately planned and carried out to draw no attention to herself; to be invisible; invisible just as she was in this society. When Jesus realised that he has been touched by a heart reaching out for him, he stopped, unwilling merely to execute impersonal healing without establishing relationship; and as he enquires about who touched him, the woman, trembling steps forward.

The story that she tells is one of shame and affliction; from childhood she suffered from continual menstrual bleeding, a condition which meant that she is, in the eyes the cult and society, permanently unclean. Jewish religion would have it that a woman, at her time of the month, is unclean and unable to participate in any act of worship or sacrifice. This woman had lived her entire life excluded from the act of atonement and sacrifice that would have made her clean in the eyes of God and the community. Condemned to a life under judgement, her conclusion and those of her neighbours was that she was under some terrible curse, some sin, for which she was being punished. Year by year, her self esteem drained away, her shame and indignity burned within her; untouchable, unmarriable; living in poverty, for she had long since spent all she had on quacks and healers who had taken her money and left her no better. She accepted without question the evaluation made on her by society; she accepted her guilt and wrongdoing and shouldered the burden for her 'failure' to be healed.

For this untouchable, one single, unseen touch would be her redemption. For while she had no trust in herself, she trusted Jesus, just as she also trusted those who judged and condemned her. She reached out to him to receive him, hopeful and optimistic that, if he saw fit, then perhaps to a worm like her, a shot of energy or a spark of power would shoot from him, enough to heal her; that without interrupting or waylaying him she, a dog, might feed off some scrap that fell from his table.

Of course, she was healed physically at that instant of physical contact; but she needed to be healed emotionally, socially and relationally. Jesus asked who had touched him, not because he needed to know, but because she and the crowd needed to hear. As she came trembling forward he reached out to her emotionally and confirmed her dignity. 'Take heart, daughter, your faith has healed you; go in peace' (Matt. 9:22). 'I accept you, I offer you my peace', he says, and not only to her but also to the crowd: you, too, now receive this woman in peace and no longer exclude her from your life. The woman on the outside is received back into the midst of the community, into relationship with God and his people.

And her freedom comes with a command: to live without guilt, to live trusting herself as healed. 'Go in peace – go with a change of mind to trust yourself to go to the temple and pray, to go into the market and buy food, to seek marriage and children and all the blessings of full membership in society. Go, trust yourself', commands Jesus, 'and be free'.

The paradox of this is that to be undefended is not to be exposed and vulnerable; rather it is, for many, to build appropriate walls around themselves and insist that others do not transgress them. It is to defend themselves properly, on the basis that God affirms them, their space in the world, and defends them.

The most wonderful, treasured and moving works of God I have ever encountered have been in working with those whose 'space in the world' has been transgressed because they did not think they could defend themselves. The work and word of God to heal and redeem them has beautifully enabled them to place boundaries around themselves, to stand tall rather than crushed.

I remember the beauty of a liturgy put together by friends with one woman. We each stood around the boundary of a circular space in the garden, in the centre of which the woman stood. The space represented herself, God's space for her in the world, his gift to her. One by one, we said 'Sorry' for the way that we, or others, had trampled across her space, ignoring her boundary, crushing her flowers, taking what we wanted. Instead, on this day, we stood at the boundary, acknowledging the space that was hers in the world, giving it back to her. For her, to be undefended was, from that day, to say 'no' to any who would trample through or walk carelessly into her space. It was to receive the 'yes' of God for her and to allow his verdict to defend her.

4.3 The Blue Hued Self

Low trust of other people; high trust of oneself

Some people grow up in relationships that are conditional. Unlike the women in the previous stories, these people have a strong sense of self. However, the extent to which they value themselves depends upon how well they can attain and maintain certain standards. Although we are familiar with this notion of conditional love or attachment, we need to observe its legacy more carefully.

To experience approval strongly on the basis of maintaining a level or reaching a standard is to be consigned to a life of unfulfilled desire. The legacy is not simply that these individuals becomes focused, disciplined and determined, although they certainly do become that. It is not simply that they become hard workers, high achievers with probably some degree of perfectionism, although they certainly will probably become that. It is not simply that they may become driven by an energy that can isolate them from others, although, once again, they may well find that this occurs.

The real legacy, the real pathology, is a fear that they are only worth what they have achieved. In childhood, the hue of Blue is knitted through the evaluations of others—perhaps a parent who express messages of disapproval towards failure or lack of conformity to the perceived or required standards. Or perhaps an oppressively evaluative educational system in which success leads to merit and status. Or perhaps a strong Christian subculture in which a kind of virtuosity is celebrated and moral failure, compromise or simply a slightly more ambivalent attitude toward discipleship is dismissed as unsatisfactory. This dissatisfaction is rarely articulated explicitly.

More often it expresses itself through informal social exclusion. There is an unspoken pecking order within the group. Those at the top do more, achieve more; those at the bottom do less.

Over the years, these criticisms and exhortations to achieve more become internalised. The adult does not need to hear them aloud; he follows them by heart. He is his own best and worst critic. Thus, a pattern of competition emerges to produce the best, only to find that the best is not good enough. This competition is endless and unwinnable because the competitor is oneself. And this competitor is formidable. He continually sets impossibly high benchmarks and standards, generally higher than those of others. Thus, instead of celebrating effort and achievement, one's best only ever points to a higher standard yet to be achieved. It is like being caught in a perpetual high jump competition, where clearing one height means that the bar will only be raised higher next time.

Gradually, the toxic emotion of fear takes a grip—a fear of failure. Usually, the person 'copes' by becoming more and more narrow, risking only high jump competitions in which they know they will be successful. They come to be 'domain masters' (in whatever field it might be), whilst avoiding the messy ambivalence and compromise of others parts of life where there is not such direct chance of success.

To continue with the metaphor of the high jump, the fear of knocking the bar off becomes increasingly disabling. Some find that they get itchy feet and need to change the scenery every few years, be it in work or otherwise. They may have a hard time settling down and being still. Others become overly controlling of their world, protecting their domain from rivals and gathering round them minions who mirror back their own superiority. Some become dominating, with a vision of endless expansion of the work they are involved in, unable to risk failure and seeing a lack of growth as a verdict of condemnation. Others become internally anxious, managing their stress inside, containing their negative emotions, trying to hold onto a world in which they are safe, soothing themselves with scripts, mantras, rituals and patterns of behaviour. Others develop a vivid fantasy life, into which they can escape from the pressure of the real life they life in; maintaining the facade of being one thing, they often have huge appetite to play out irresponsibility, power and freedom in the apparently consequence-free world of their mind, or the internet.

The pathology underlying all of these behaviours is the same. It is not, as the Christian world has so often depicted it, a problem of 'lust' or 'greed'. These are labels which the guilt narrative applies with abandon. Instead, it is a pathology of fear—fear that their fundamental self-worth is composed exclusively of maintaining certain standards in their lives. They do not trust that others will want them, accept them, tolerate them and love them for who they are. They are never enough. They do not enjoy a life of settled contentment, a gift to all those who allow themselves to be known and loved by God.

To live this life is to live perpetually disappointed. Nothing one does or achieves is enough. Nothing satisfies. No goal, once reached, offers the pleasure it promised. No target, once attained, allows celebration. Work is not followed by rest; the slower day never arrives. Thus, most experience periodic burn-out or crashes when the unsustainable pace collapses. Some only relax in sleep; some are prone to cycles of illness; some are on anxiety-related drugs; some are always ill, with weakened immune systems; some compartmentalise their lives, becoming superficial and atomised people who deny their mistakes and conceal their weaknesses; and some live in a small worlds which only they control, becoming obsessive over any threat or change.

For these individuals, the pleasure of the present moment is never available. Life is lived in a perpetual future that never arrives. The present moment is entered and experienced only as a means to attain a future. The taste of food, the salary earned, the gift received, the accolade awarded—all are merely stashed away in the reservoir or resources required to propel one forward to the next gain. Life is commoditised. It is no wonder that they end up valuing others as utilities, units to get jobs done. It is no wonder that they approve of those who are efficient and productive and disapprove of the 'indolent and self-indulgent'. It is no wonder they look down (secretly perhaps) on those without their stamina, mental discipline and self-sacrifice. And it is no wonder those around them both admire them and fear them.

But theirs is a world that is lonely and often hard to reach. Their hearts are often hidden away and untended. Ironically, they are the people who we often choose to lead our churches, applauding them for their success in growing ministries for the kingdom. For we, like them, also buy into the myth of utility, choosing to believe that God is the Great Chief Executive, recruiting only the most talented, committed, influential and able Chief Operating Officers to run his mission on earth. Which of us, for example, would have turned away a man of such talent, position, integrity and wealth as Jesus did in the story below?

The man who trusted himself, but not others

Our third story concerns a young man who represented all that the previous women were not. He was wealthy, a sign—in those days, it was believed—of God's blessing. He was young and powerful, good and upright, well-known for his righteousness and moral life. This fine, upstanding young man, in whom are manifest all the blessings of a life lived under God, comes to Jesus. He has come to enquire about how to gain eternal life. Jesus replies that he is sure the man already knows what he needs to do: he must keep the commandments—love your neighbour, honour your father and mother, and so on. The man quickly replies that all these he has kept since he was a boy.

All these he has kept since he was a boy...When you think about it, that is quite a claim—to have kept the commands of God from childhood all the way through to early adulthood. This young man demonstrates a lack of awareness of himself and of the human condition; the kind of over-confident naïvety one finds in a child who boldly proclaims that they are going to be the first person to fly to Mars, or swim across the Atlantic Ocean. Mature people, who have lived long enough and looked hard enough, know all too well that, despite their best efforts, their lives have fallen far short of the ideals even they set themselves in their youth.

This young man has yet to reach that self-understanding; his world is still propped up by the ideals of benchmarks and targets, rules and boundaries by which—although they may be morally good in a ritualistic and external sort of way—a naïve, young person might come to think that they have been obedient. He has either set up such limited, external rules that he can legitimately claim to have maintained them, or he has been unaware of the pervasive, eroding compromises he makes—that we all make—on a daily basis to shape a world in our own image and fashion a life on our own, personal and ultimately selfish terms.

We are told that Jesus, when he hears this reply, looks at the man and 'loves him'. He sees and knows where the young man is, even if the young man does not. Jesus tells him starkly to go and sell all he has, to give to the poor, to come and follow him. Then, Jesus says, this young man will receive treasures in heaven. Sadly, for this young man, only radical surgery can removed the self-deceit and self-sufficiency that has taken hold of him. He knows he lacks something, but ultimately the young man thinks that only he knows the answers, only he can set the standards—no-one else. So, even though he asks, 'What must I do?', he is not ready to listen. He already knows. He trusts himself and no-one else to set the direction. Sadly, this young man is very far from the kingdom of heaven. This trust of self keeps him from the kingdom, keeps him from rest and keeps him from relationship. As Jesus says, how hard it is for the rich to enter the kingdom of heaven!

For the kingdom of heaven is not a matter of self-righteousness and self-belief but of dependence and trust in Another. The call to sell all he had is not a universal call for all followers of Christ to live in poverty, but a call to this particular young man to let go of all that he relies on. For him, it is less the money and more what it represents— the status it affords him, the righteousness it mirrors back to him, the control it gives him. It is to let go of all of this and, in a new kind of dependency and vulnerability, trust himself instead to the care of Jesus.

For the man or woman who trusts in himself or herself, the path to redemption is hard for it involves relinquishing this very trust in self and placing it in another. This is something this kind of person has learned not to do. Their whole lives are orientated around self-protection, and self-control (in the literal sense). They live their lives by self-determined standards and judge themselves as personal critics. They will live or die by their own judgement and ward off vulnerability and defeat by continually acquiring the things they need to succeed or remain safe in themselves. How hard it is for the rich to enter the kingdom of heaven!

What a shock we find it, that the gathering of skills, competencies, experiences and qualifications to make us rich, actually make it harder for us to become free. Instead they ensnare us in a life of isolation and self-protection, unable to risk the vulnerability of truly trusting ourselves to another. Thus, they lead out of fear and by control. This young man, we are told, when he heard what Jesus had to say to him, went away sad, unable to receive the gift of life Jesus had to offer. Receiving is the very thing this kind of person does not know how to do.

4.4 The Red Hued Self

High trust of other people and high trust of oneself

Conventional wisdom would have it that, in a model with four categories, where three are in some ways problematic, the fourth is the one in which the problems are resolved. The win-win situation, the best of all worlds. Thus it would seem with this model. In our matrix of trust, the wool of this self is woven in high trust—high trust of oneself and of others. The Red Hued self—what better, warmer, richer, more secure combination could there be? Free from the anxieties that people only value you for what you do. Free from the fear that relationships with others are about to break. Free from the suspicions that others will let you down.

In one sense, this is certainly the case. For these individuals, the world seems basically safe. Unsurprisingly, this breeds a kind of confidence and assurance. In relation to the fear narrative, these individuals seem the least exposed to the toxicology of a fallen world. Affection and acceptance have been available consistently in this environment. Within the context of the Gospel, one may be left wondering what good news is left for this individual to receive? If you insist, as I have, that the Gospel must offer good news for our entire posture in the world, then what deficit, what legacy of fear, does this individual need to be saved from?

Perhaps the most obvious is the fear of fear itself. For those who have come to experience their world as basically safe, the fear of being unsafe or of their loved ones being unsafe can be very strong. Psychologists talk of the problem of those who seek to 'rescue' others. Rescuing is the act of saving another person from their situation. Red Hued people are often compulsive rescuers. They find it difficult to allow other people to struggle or to be in pain because such experiences are unfamiliar to them. And, of course, because they are 'secure' individuals, they are often seen as having broad shoulders by others: I know of many 'Red Hued' people who carry vast numbers of dependents on their shoulders, dependents who are thrilled to have found a rescuer. After all, many of us would love someone to come and make our lives better and sort out our problems. However, it does not necessarily help us grow up and take responsibility ourselves.

Indeed, one of the issues of the Red Hued self is the struggle fully to grow up into adult selves. Again, to deploy a helpful bit of psychological language known as Transactional Analysis, their sense of safety in the world comes from (probably) their parental relationship in which they, the Child, are secured by the Parent (as a psychological type). This unqualified attachment extends into their adult selves and defines the basic posture in which they bring themselves into relationships. They either know themselves as Child to another's Parent, or as Parent to another's Child. Parents rescue and protect children – thus they rescue and protect other adults who, abdicating responsibility, choose to be 'Child' in the relationship.

This patterning becomes painfully exposed at the death of the original Parent. This is a loss which I have observed numerous Red-Hued individuals negotiate in later life. The Parent dies at a good age, not out of turn, when their child is now a mature grown-up, perhaps in middle age. The mature child, who has adopted the posture of Parent predominately throughout their adult life is known as a secure, confident assured person and one expects someone so psychologically well adjusted and robust to negotiate this loss in a healthy and non-traumatic way. However, one often finds that they struggle unexpectedly, being quite thrown by the loss of this individual relationship even at a late stage of life. The reason for this, of course, is that in this death, the Child loses the Parent. There is a sense in which this person still has within them the child who has not grown up, who is still emotionally secured by an attachment to the other. When that attachment is severed, the child experiences this as abandonment. It is a powerful, disturbing exposure, leaving the adult vulnerable and alone in the world.

The best human relationships are not secure or robust enough to 'redeem' us. The failure of human attachment in the face of death renders the most healthy parent-child relationship deficient in its power to set us free. Not only this, but it can also lead to other pathologies along the way. I have witnessed repeated poor judgement in leaders who are (psychometrically tested to be) Red Hued. They repeatedly over-trust people, seeing the best in them, naïvely assuming that others will be as good as their word. This is often not the case and it results in all manner of misunderstanding, and indeed an unwillingness to confront people who are behaving inappropriately. Not only this, but they often promise too much, believing that they are able to 'overcome problems' and 'make it all work out'. Glossed with a spiritual position of 'pastor' or 'prophet' it does not take much for their followers to 'believe too much' only to be colossally disappointed by the inevitable failure of their leader to deliver what they had hoped for. There is an inappropriate sense of power and efficacy which this individual must shake off. Often this only comes with a crushing experience of their weakness and powerlessness. They must learn to live in a world which is 'unsafe' in order properly to help others who are unsafe.

There is also a possibility of more narcissistic and even sociopathic behaviour. Our sensitivity and empathy toward others is related to our own experience of the pain we see other people suffering. If we have not experienced such pain, we may not develop the empathy to feel for other people. In a mild form, this can just result in a kind of superficiality, a sort of casualness toward others, a thick-skinnedness, or lack of understanding about just how hurt and upset other people really are. To be Red Hued is to be rubbery; things bounce off.

There is also no doubt that more extreme forms of negative social behaviour—and even sociopathic behaviour—can result from an inappropriately inflated view of self. The truth is that not all our actions are to be unconditionally sanctioned, even as a child. The truth is that there is a measure of disapproval that all children need to experience to form a healthy sense of their own limits and boundaries. To be without these is to become like Narcissus, self-loving, living in a myth of our own self-love. A lack of empathy for others due to an inflated view of oneself creates the possibility of treating other human beings as objects. Objectifying the other is always the first step toward misuse and then abuse.

The man who trusted himself and others

The fourth and final story stretches throughout the Gospel accounts and involves Jesus' relationship with a man called Simon. Simon was a fisherman and an early follower of Jesus. He was, to some extent, the self-appointed spokesman, even leader, of the small gang of intimate men who came to be known as Jesus' apostles. Simon demonstrated a character fit for leadership and it was for that reason that Jesus gave him a new name—Peter, from Petros meaning 'rock'.

Peter was bold, confident, optimistic and positive. Whenever a challenge presented itself, Peter was the first to propose they take it on, and head on. Peter was rarely troubled by self-doubt. He said things that made others cringe; he made many faux pas and blunders. In short, he risked appearing stupid. Like the time when Jesus came to them walking on water and Peter, quick as a flash, asked to come to him—to walk on water! A man who was not slow to ask to walk on water, not deferential in requesting the best and most adrenaline-filled experience around and not shy of putting himself forward ahead of others.

A man, too, who was not slow to trust Jesus: where others were hesitant and cautious, Peter was bold. He had worked out early on that Jesus was pretty special and that was enough for him; he would back him, just like he backed himself. Peter was the great 'backer'; when Jesus suggested his apostles would desert him, Peter asserted he would never do such a thing! Others might fail in faith, but not him! He was confident of it! He would always back Jesus and he would always back himself in a tight fix; it was no surprise that it was Peter who flashed his sword when Jesus came to be arrested, a gesture which Jesus indicated missed the point of the time that was now at hand.

Later on the night of Jesus' arrest, after that brief violent resistance, in the early hours, in a courtyard belonging to the high priest, Peter was to encounter a side of him of which he knew very little. Jesus had forewarned him that, on this very night, he would betray him—three times in fact—before the cock crowed and the new day dawned. Thus it happened. With Jesus inside, arrested, being questioned, on trial for his life, Peter slunk in through the courtyard gate and lurked in the shadows hoping to hear what was going on, unnoticed.

But as he later warmed himself by the fire he was spotted, recognised. 'Wasn't he a follower of this man, this Galilean?', a servant girl asked. 'Wasn't he a disciple of this Jesus?', someone else asked. Three times they asked if he knew Jesus. Three times Peter swore that he did not. Three times he was given the chance to bear witness to his trust in Jesus, and three times he balked, frozen perhaps with fear for the first time. Perhaps for the first time, Peter's own bravado and self-confidence reached its end. Perhaps, confused by the apparent weakness of Jesus and his refusal to flee, Peter discovered what it meant to be alone. The chord that had bound him to Jesus, that had led him safely across the waves of the sea that other night towards Jesus, was broken; Jesus had gone and he was alone, utterly alone. He was unprotected, weak and lost. Suddenly he discovered his fragility and his fear. Cornered and terrified, lashing out was the only thing to do.

However, Peter was to discover that the relationship with God is not like another human relationship. God reserves the prerogative to mystery and absence. It is in Him to be beyond us, and whilst Peter sought to contain Jesus within the references of normal human relationships, he was to discover that powerlessness, sacrifice and even death were to be embraced by the divine. Jesus loved Peter and had not deserted him. In fact, the very act that led Jesus to that courtyard was the act of self-sacrifice that would be, for Peter and all others, the act of salvation and atonement. For Peter, who had a trust and confidence in Jesus the man, this was the moment when he was called to trust in Jesus, his God.

It was several days later that they, Jesus and Peter, met again on a beach in Galilee. Peter had returned to his old trade of fishing and Jesus, the risen Jesus, waited for him on the shore. The meeting was poignant, full of meaning and unspoken emotion. The purpose was reconciliation. Peter needed to be given and to receive forgiveness. But he was also given a call—a call to feed Jesus' lambs, his followers, his church. The shepherd was entrusting the protection of his flock to Peter. And he also foretold a future that would end in Peter's own death, a death that mirrored Jesus' own, with his own arms stretched out, in weakness and vulnerability.

Jesus' offer to Peter of reconciliation was also an invitation into a new kind of life. A life lived not out of trusting his own judgement, but in walking humbly with his God, walking down a path of dependency and vulnerability. Peter was to discover that life involved the freedom not to defend oneself. This freedom was big enough to encounter death and not be overcome. This freedom came from being secured by the presence, the attachment and the unconditional regard of God. This freedom would tie Peter in his life and in his death to Christ. Heaven would prove to be nothing more than the intimate extension of the same attachment Peter had come to know on earth, free from fear or pain or sorrow or loss. Jesus came to set Peter free—free to serve, free to lead his church.

It seems that within the fallen human condition there is no experience of relationship or attachment that is sufficient to redeem us. The narrative of fear is complex, leading to subtle psychological topographies which need to be depicted carefully. Fear, as a root, results in interweaving strands of behaviour as varied as greed, violence, self-harm, conscientiousness, moral duty, guilt, attention-seeking, apparent altruism, lust, anxiety, compliance, defiance, and so on.

This is no one-dimensional account of human behaviour. Nor is it superficially or merely looking at behaviour. Nor is it simply psychological, divorced from either the wider social context of our formation, nor the environmental context of our history, nor the spiritual context of anthropology. The fear narrative is a sufficient axis upon which to tease out the subtleties of the human condition. It suggests that all human needs (love, self realisation, belonging) are valid, but are contingent upon and subordinate to this deeper root cause. It suggests that other 'sins' (greed, lust, envy, anger, etc) are also derivative of from this fundamental root. Each of these others, whilst adding their own texture and tone, is coloured by this earlier, basic archetype. To resolve the human condition is to resolve this basic condition of fear.

Chapter 5

The Centrality of Adoption

"When you pray, do not keep on babbling like pagans, for they think they will be heard because of their many words. Do not be like them, for your Father knows what you need before you ask him.

So do not worry, saying, 'What shall we eat?' or 'What shall we drink?' or 'What shall we wear?' For the pagans run after all these things, and your heavenly Father knows that you need them. But seek first his kingdom and his righteousness, and all these things will be given to you as well."

Matthew 6.7-8, 31-3

I have suggested that, since the fault line of mistrust in the Genesis 3 story, human beings have experienced the world as basically unsafe. I have also suggested that the condition of fear that flows from this is an outworking of both our relative scale and the reality of time; the future is unknown. Thus, human behaviour is always, to some extent, future orientated. By this I mean that human behaviour is an attempt by an individual, acting in the present moment, to make her future more secure than it may be otherwise.

It is easy to see how many of our big decisions relate to our future. Where will we go to university? Which job should we take? Where should we live? But even this applies to the smaller decisions as well—how much we save, how we plan our diaries, where we will take holidays. We can go further—how we look after ourselves, when we go to sleep, when we wake—and still we find the same pattern.

In fact, even our more subtle psychological behaviours also function in this way. I tend to smile at people when I talk because I have learned that they will probably smile back at me and this leaves the conversation feeling a little better as a result. My smile is a gesture which 'reaches into the future' (a matter of a second or two in this case) to secure the kind of future I prefer (one in which they are happy with themselves and me). Similarly, I tend to be self-depreciating because I have learned that it often secures a compliment. 'I really made a bit of a mess of that presentation' may often be followed by 'Oh no, far from it, it was a great success'. My behaviour, whether subtle or obvious, helps to secure a more favourable future.

That is one of the reasons why the theology of God's adoption in the New Testament is so central to the redemption of the narrative of fear. We have sketched a few dimensions in the Old Testament of God's invitation to his people to abandon a posture of fear and the associated religious rituals of idolatry in favour of trusting that he, YHWH, will secure their future for them. This theology of fear and safety is, now, brought to its climax in Jesus' teaching about the nature of the Kingdom in Matthew 6. Prayer is the appropriate posture in which creatures relate to their creator. Therefore, Jesus' teaching is fundamentally about the character of this relationship.

'Do not be like the pagans or the hypocrites', says Jesus. The pagans babble with lots of words—why? Because, the pagan inhabits a world in which the capricious gods can somehow, through a multitude of words, sacrifices, rituals, etc, be cajoled into offering favour. The fear narrative.

Do not be like the hypocrites, who fast and perform a visible theatre of devotion before a watching audience. Do not seek the positive affirmation from your human audience; do not seek to make yourself safe in the world by securing the favour of those other human beings around you. The fear narrative......

Instead, pray to God as Father........

This language of God as Father is radically new. God is described as almighty, as creator, as protector, as provider, even as YHWH, but rarely up to this point as Father. It is the understanding of God as Father that is so central to the Kingdom of heaven, the kingdom that Jesus proclaims as very near. In this kingdom, we are to understand and experience ourselves as children; we are to understand our identity as those who, in dependency and vulnerability, trust ourselves to the divine goodness of God as Father. And it is this understanding that ultimately defines who is in and who is outside the Kingdom— those who know God as Father and those who do not. 'When you pray, pray to your Father.' Because God is our Father, we can adopt a new posture; we can live in a kind of freedom and fearlessness. 'For your Father knows what you need before you ask him.' Truly, this adoption will have ramifications in every area of our lives.

Prayer, for example. Prayer is no longer the means of recruiting God to our cause. Prayer is transformed into our participation into the movements of God. 'Our Father in heaven, hallowed be your name, your kingdom come your will be done...'

Finances, for example. 'Do not store up for yourself treasure on earth', for your contentment does not lie in more stuff or relationships or achievements. Rather, it lies in seeking the riches of the Kingdom. We have tended to see these riches as a future, eschatological reward for today's investment. However, Jesus invites us to a life of abundance here and now. 'I have come that you have life and have it to the full.' The Kingdom of God is available to us now. We can both invest and enjoy rich fruit now.

Providence, for example. This Kingdom life offers us the riches of freedom from fear and worry. 'Do not worry about what you will eat or what you will drink or what you will wear' for the pagans (those who do not know God as Father) worry about all these things. Do not live in the fear narrative, exposed to the continual vagaries and uncertainties of tomorrow, consumed by whether you will have enough, absorbed by mechanisms that will allow you to invest and save enough. Instead, 'seek first the Kingdom, and all these things will be given you as well'. For the Kingdom is the giving of all things to us in the generous abundance of a divine father providing for his children.

I have suggested that the narrative of fear is the driving influence of who we have allowed ourselves to become. Thus, our behaviours, emotions and what we call our personality are all bound up with our rebellion against God. Fear is woven throughout us and, therefore, the Gospel must offer a means by which this narrative of fear is unpicked. It is not simply a matter of putting the garment in the general washing machine of God's redemptive processes—this will not remove the thread. Nor can the garment just be dyed in a similar process. No, the work required is more fundamental and much more personal. Instead, the garment must be re-stitched. The Gospel must involve the specific, intimate and tender re-working of our personal fabric by the fingers of God such that our very selves begin to depict trust, security and freedom in their very fibres. Philosophically as well as psychologically, the Gospel must go back to the source, healing those foundational relationships of attachment, beginning with our parental attachments.

God, as Father, is central to our redemption. And in this sense, Fatherhood also includes Motherhood. God's ability to redeem our tattered, knotted, discoloured fabric of self relies upon his inviting us into a new kind of secure, intimate parental attachment, a fabric which is whole, which can begin to heal the deficits of our human experience of being parented which we all have had to some extent.

I must be careful that I am not misheard here. I am not suggesting that coming into relationship with God as Father primarily results in the healing of our human relationships with our genetic (or adopted) parents, although that can happen. Rather, I am suggesting that our redemption as individuals fundamentally relies upon experiencing a relationship with God as Father (and Mother). It is only such a divine relationship that can heal, resolve and restore dysfunctions in life, which may have resulted from deficits in those natural relationships. The experience of attachment with our parents is determinative, although not exclusively so, in the formation of the fabric of who we have become. To this extent, then, its particular influence must be re-stitched.

I believe this is why the apostle Paul locates adoption at the very heart of the transition from being one of the pagans to being one of the saints, from being led by the flesh to being led by the Spirit. For, it is in the Spirit that we have the spirit of Sonship (and we can appropriately in today's context say Daughtership) rather than a spirit of slavery and fear. 'Those who are led by the Spirit', he says, 'are sons of God, no longer slaves to fear...And by him (the spirit) we cry Abba, Father.' God no longer calls us slaves, but children, and we call him Father. This transition from slaves to children, from orphans to heirs, provides us not merely with psychological intimacy. It also allows us a new intimacy of communication with God, through the spirit, in deep words beyond language.

It also provides us with cosmological safety. There is, climaxes Paul at the end of his expanding narrative of the redemptive purposes and movements of God in the letter to the Roman church, 'nothing which can separate us from the love of God'. Our lives are secure. More than that, our futures are secure. The child of God can now go forth in the world confidently, devoid of fear; the basic threat of hostility has been overcome. God is now for us; and he is for us as Father.

Chapter 6

Paul and the Theology of the Cross

"Everyone exists in the very nature of suffering, so to abuse or mistreat each other is futile. The foundation of all spiritual practice is love."

Dalai Lama

6.1 The Cross: Symbol of Reconciliation

For Paul, the cross is supremely an event of reconciliation. It is the hostility of God that must primarily be dealt with if the curse in the fallen world is to be revoked and healed. Paul's language of 'peace' through the cross has often been heard only through the narrative of guilt. We were guilty, but God's son took the punishment instead. Because of this sacrifice the debt has been paid. God is no longer angry with us and we are saved from a future of fire and brimstone.

Although this is true, our reconciliation with God is more than a relenting of God's anger. Reconciliation is also the reorientation of God to us as benevolent Father; this puts the removal of fear at the heart of the Gospel transformation.

We have tended to draw a distinction between this initial reconciliation, and the reconciliation of our daily living, seeing redemption and sanctification as a two-step process. The first 'puts us right with God'; the second is the means by which we live our lives changed by that truth, often through our own efforts.

However, as we come to understand sin as our attempts to make ourselves safe, the line between the initial and the daily reconciliations begins to fade. I have suggested earlier that the root or central thread of our sin is fear, fear of God and fear of potential threat which finds expression in our relationships. Thus, the way we are reconciled with God is the key to our ongoing sanctification. Because we are now safe, fear no longer needs to be a factor in our relationships. We are sanctified as we allow ourselves to be caught up in this truth.

This implies that there is actually little distinction—no stage one and then stage two. We are not first rescued by the cross, only then to try to live out the life fit for the forgiven. No—we are saved, decisively and singularly. Because God draws near as Father, we are saved from the threat and hostility that we have feared. God is both all-powerful and 'for us' once more. We can now live in this world in trusting, open, undefended relationships.

A symbol of peace in our situations and relationships

Jesus' death and resurrection brings us peace. 'My peace I give you, my peace I leave with you' (John 14: 27).

Peace is the central fruit of the transition from one status to another. At an emotional level, we can experience a loss of the anxiety and stress required to maintain our systems of defence. At a sociological level, we can now engage with others as friends rather than as threats or commodities.

Jesus is the one who 'has broken down the dividing wall of hostility, making the two one' (Ephesians 2: 14). Paul gives us a picture of what this looks like in Galatians: 'for now there is neither Jew nor Greek, male nor female, slave nor free—you are all one in Christ' (Galatians 3: 28).

This social peace is not the result of human effort to be nicer, kinder people, to put up with people we do not really like, or to imitate Christ who loved even the unlovely. No, it is the basic willingness of the people of God to experience each other as neither threats nor commodities, but rather as friends or as family.

Seeing others as a gift rather than a threat or commodity is not like putting on rose-tinted spectacles. It is not an act of will or a leap of the imagination to see the best in people. Nor should it be something that is particularly difficult, although some may find it so. It is a choice. It is a choice to be still, a choice to live in and embrace the world as God now gives it to us—as a gift.

We can now receive people and situations openly because the Father is for us. We have nothing to fear. We, like little children, can encounter and receive the world and all that it contains—every day, every hour, every moment—as a gift. This is not something that is only sometimes true. The question for us is whether we will receive this truth and participate in it—each day, each moment. Will we choose to live by the Spirit, finding our safety as His child, or will we continue to try to make our own way to safety?

6.2 What Really is 'Life by the Spirit'?

We have said that the cross is a symbol of our reconciliation with God as Father. That act of reconciliation deals with our fear and brings peace when we first believe and, in our daily lives, as we believe that truth more and more. It is in the daily living that Paul contrasts the person who lives by the flesh and cannot please God with the person 'controlled by the Spirit, whose life is peace'.

How 'life by the Spirit' is often interpreted

A common interpretation is that we, by the power of the Spirit, are being slowly enabled to live more and more Christ-like lives. This process is long and slow and it involves our commitment. This 'commitment' often translates into a striving to live up the high ideals of the Christ-like life, but always falling short. Previously, when we were 'dead to sin' or 'in the flesh', none of our actions or thoughts were ever pleasing to God. Now, in Christ, it becomes possible for us to start to please God and, by the Spirit as a kind of agency or force within us, we are able to do so more and more in our lives. This experience of life in Christ seems rather like a mixed sack of grain. Rotten grains are gradually replaced with good grains, but the sack always remains mixed. We battle with cycles of guilt and then forgiveness. However, thanks to God, Jesus Christ has freed us from condemnation.

Is this what Paul means by 'life by the Spirit'?

Paul however, does not describe the phenomenon of 'being in the

Spirit' in these terms. He does not say, 'The person in the Spirit will begin to please God as the power of the Spirit works in him'. Rather than the future tense, Paul uses the present tense. He asserts that the person who lives according to the Spirit is 'controlled by the Spirit of God' and that his mind is one of life and peace' (Romans 8: 5-8).

But who can live such a life? Who has ever had such a pure, unmixed, singular mind of life and peace? The key to understanding this is to understand that when Paul refers to 'the flesh', 'the body', 'sinful man' or 'law of death' (terms he uses almost interchangeably) he is not talking about some condition within us but rather a realm outside and around us. We have tended, in the guilt narrative, to see sin as a kind of infection, which has rendered all our bodies sick, corrupting our flesh and condemning us to die under the judgement of the law. But Paul here speaks of the kind of world that we have inhabited. He is talking of a cosmology under which we have been toiling (and dying).

When Paul talks of the 'law of death' and the 'law of the Spirit' this is best understood as the 'realm of the law'. There are two realms that exist: one is the 'realm of the law' which condemns us under the fear narrative. It judges us; we fall short; we live in fear of retribution; we live anticipating the hostile reaction of the God in the Garden. We hide; we conceal; we project and protect in order to try to be safe. We live locked in a world ruled by fear, unable to please God, unable to do anything other than behave in a way that is defended.

The 'realm of the Spirit', however, is not based on fear but on adoption. We 'received the Spirit of sonship. And by him we cry, Abba, Father' (Romans 8: 15). This is another space, another world which has been brought into reality through the death of Jesus, the divine Son. A new space, a new narrative has been opened up in the world where we are not condemned by fear. To step into this world is to step away from the slavery of fear into freedom. It is to live with a mind of 'life and peace' rather than death and fear.

Paul is not talking about sources of power to live out a life (in other words, the inadequate power of the Law of Moses versus the adequate power of the Spirit in Christ). Instead, Paul is talking about the space of fear versus the space of safety. He is depicting a new cosmology in which the divine is presented as Father, who is for us. From this cosmology there flows a new anthropology, one in which human beings can live in trust, peace and life towards this God and towards one another. The mind in the Spirit is life and peace, not because of our efforts and determination, but because there is no longer anything to be afraid about. Hence Paul can conclude this great section with the statement, 'If God is for us, who can be against us?' (Romans 8: 31).

In this depiction, the choice of living 'in the flesh' or ' in the Spirit' is not to be understood as some internal battle between the bit of us that is sanctified and wants to please God and the bit of us that is still sinful and harks back to the old days. This is not the struggle to allow God to slice more of the egg white away from the yolk. Rather, it is the option to choose which space to live in: to live in the fear of the flesh or to live in the peace the Spirit.

Part II

Embracing an Undefended Life

Chapter 7

Describing the Characteristics of the Undefended Life

"If a man wishes to be sure of the road he treads on, he must close his eyes and walk in the dark."

St John of the Cross

7.1 The Two Spaces

Living in the Spirit is only and is always life and peace. It offers no other experience of self and the world. It transfigures all reality, be that suffering, loss, pain, joy, success or failure, into an experience of 'gift' in which we encounter the love of the divine Father for us. It renders all power which can come against us as impotent—be that bankruptcy, homelessness, rejection, hostility, hunger or opposition. No thing can reconfigure this world again as threat. The threat of the world has been disarmed.

It is the potency of this reality and the security of this posture that led Dallas Willard, in The Divine Conspiracy, to conclude that when Jesus asked for forgiveness for his crucifiers as he hung from the tree, it was not a difficult but rather an easy thing for him to do.[1] Willard is right. For in the Spirit the mind is controlled by life and peace.

---

1   Dallas Willard, *The Divine Conspiracy* (Harper One, 1998), p. 183

To be 'in the Spirit' is not a kind of mystical state, nor is it an act of supernaturally empowered will. It is a place where the mind is free of animosity, free of hostility, free of fear. When we are in the Spirit, love flows from us easily, abundantly, like a gushing torrent, towards the world that is 'in the flesh'. The guilt narrative leads us to look in disbelief at Jesus' kindness, mercy and grace on the cross to those persecutors. We are amazed at his capacity to forgive and love. Faced with similar circumstances, we know that we would have cursed and sworn bitter revenge. We hope and pray that should anything terrible ever happen to us, we might be given the inner grace to find forgiveness in our hearts.

But these images are unhelpful. This image of 'praying that our mean hearts will be filled', that we will have more power or grace within us as if it were some liquid refreshment, is unhelpful. It leads us to focus inwardly, to become preoccupied with our own, internal pathology. It leads us to enquire and then seek to muster the capacity inside us to be kind and good, with God as the source of our empowerment. It leads us to feel insecure and guilty when we cannot or do not behave in that way. It leads us to feel inadequate—poor Christians with whom God has a lot of work left to do.

Two spaces we can live in now

That, of course, may indeed be the case, but our posture should not be towards being 'more filled with the love of God' (in the kind of liquid metaphor way) but rather to 'live more fully in the life of God' (in the spatial metaphor kind of way). There are two spaces we can live in: the flesh and the Spirit. The truth is that most of us (including me) choose to live most of our lives in the flesh. We live in the fear narrative. In this space, we live out our pathology, depicting ourselves in a way that makes us safe, on our own familiar terms. This depiction is what we tend to call our personality. We try, if we are religious, to wrench this self toward kinder, benign behaviours, but it does not work.

This self exists in fear, it is woven in fear, it is coordinated to achieve a certain purpose. It cannot abandon that purpose. It cannot simply cease to use those strategies in order to 'serve another God'; to do so would render it psychologically and socially vulnerable. Thus, our attempts are fraught with frustration, disappointment and guilt. We plead with God, co-opting him to our cause, hoping that he will help us stop being an angry person, to deal with our anxiety, to take away our guilt, and to become more patient, kind, tolerant, loving, merciful and generous. But he does not answer.

In the end, we settle for a compromise. We rework some aspects of this self with a new Christian thread—language, costumes, scripts and stories that are acceptable to the Christian audience. We learn the ways of securing a favourable response from the Christian critics. We sort out some of the obvious and easy knots and tangles—obvious misdeeds like tax evasion, bad language, adultery and pornography. We add on some easy virtues—good time management, serving in Sunday school and some financial giving.

Gradually, after a few years, we have it figured out and our fabric looks pretty much like anyone else's in the church. We now avoid the social shame of looking 'different' from the others when we turn up to church. We also help newcomers conform to this social pattern when they 'come into the church from the world', thereby eliminating the awkward discrepancies of tone and hue in our church community. We send those with too radical a pattern out to the mission field where the call to be 'different' is a prerequisite.

With this personal re-weaving having gone so far, we settle down into a familiar routine of church attendance and bible reading, wondering over the decades whether we misread the ideology of radical transformation in the New Testament in the zeal of our youth.

The defended life is found in church just as it is in the wider world. The defended life, the life in the flesh, the body—all interchangeable terms—is that life ruled by the fear narrative. It has nothing to do with eternal life. Eternal life, as depicted by Jesus is to live in a space where we are secured by the love of our divine Father in each moment. In this posture, 'in the Spirit', we experience freedom.

The daily choice to participate

This way of being in the world is available to us on a moment-by-moment basis. It is there. It is a world that is within our reach; it is a reality that is simply veiled to us. It exists alongside this world of the flesh, drawing us into it, inviting us into its safety. We know when we have been there; we feel it like electricity. It is like extending a hand toward a mirror, only to discover that the surface of the mirror ripples and bends as our hand passes straight through. The self-referential world opens up for us and we pass beyond into another kind of world and space. We tentatively reach forward, stepping into this world, and as we do so we find ourselves breathing new air.

This way of being in peace continues as we remain on the other side of the mirror. The day unfolds not in an anxious, fretful series of tasks and obligations, some endured, some enjoyed. It is not a race to cram productivity into our day and feel powerful at the end of it. Instead, the day is received as it is given. Without fear, our financial situation no longer requires that gripping, constant attention and planning whereby we worry over the latest economic forecasts and our potential bonus or job security. Instead, we acknowledge the financial resources we have for the moment, the day, the month, the year.

We acknowledge what we need for the 'now', the 'today' that Jesus talks about in Matthew 6—be it a day or a year. And we locate our attention on the goodness of our divine Father, receiving the assurance that He will provide all we need. We choose to let go of the aspiration to own this house or that, to gain this promotion or that, to be in this relationship or that. We choose to let go of the fearful fantasy of whether we could cope if we defaulted on our mortgage repayments and lost our home. We choose to embrace freedom in the reality that the Father knows our needs and will provide for us. We relish his love and the intimacy with which he knows our situation. We anticipate the little joys he will give us along the way as he meets our needs, the unexpected delights, the 'more than enough's he will gift to us. We wait to see how things will unfurl and to receive them gratefully in their time.

We choose to breathe more slowly, to take everything available from each breath. We entrust ourselves to the adventure of being a child of the divine Father and acknowledge the absolute absurdity of the Gospel: God in Christ asserts that 'he is for us' and that we are, in him, safe. This gospel breaks the narrative of fear that has ruled our lives; this gospel invites us to receive and enjoy eternal in the Spirit, now, in this moment.

In this space, for these moments, we are free. We are in peace. However, we live in this space, inhabit this world beyond the mirror, very rarely. For a moment or two later we find ourselves wrenched back, hauled through the liquid glass, which closes and becomes solid again. Once more, we find ourselves facing a world which is uncertain and perilous. Our precious peace is quashed by the sheer realities of life and our fragile stillness; it is terrorised by our racing minds which try to manage the demands of the day. In this sealed world, our pattern of behaviour is inevitable, as predictable as the chiming of a clock. In this world, we begin once again the subtle, arduous, endless task of managing an unsafe existence with our old familiar strategies. There are times when this life feels benign, tolerable, pleasant and even fulfilling; and we wonder whether there is any need to seek another kind of way to be in the world. And then there are other times when this world collapses into toxicity, rendering our best hopes poisoned, fulfilling nothing, producing (as Eliot describes) only the 'bitter tastelessness of shadow fruit'.

The common Christian experience of living a life that is only very partially consonant with the work of the Spirit is explained not in terms of the 'mixed bag of grain' metaphor but rather in terms of the mixed cosmology in which we still live. The 'now and then not yet' is the co-existence of two realms: the realm of the Spirit and the realm of the flesh. These realms are not so much vertically located (earth / flesh below and heaven / Spirit above) as we sometime might think; nor are they chronologically related (earth now and heaven later). They are horizontally related, existing alongside one another in continual intersection.

The experience of the Christian person is the experience of being able to pass through the veil, to touch and indeed to participate in the realm of the Spirit concurrently with one's life here and now. This option does not involve removing ourselves to particular physical places (although the legacy of spiritual openness in some historic praying communities makes the air 'thin' in those places certainly), but it rather involves becoming aware of the intersecting movements of God, in his Spirit, in the time and the space in which we find ourselves. It is to this ongoing experience that we must now turn.

7.2 Life as Gift

What does it look like to abandon the fear narrative and to embrace the freedom of our divine Father? What kind of experience of life does it open up? How does the world look different? In what ways do one's daily activities change? In other words, what are the characteristics, or the phenomena, of living the undefended life—the life in the Spirit? Four central characteristics of this new life are: the ability to live life as a gift, living in the present moment, relinquishing control, but taking responsibility, and taking risks.

The first movement involves the choice to experience our life as gift. This is harder than it looks. For a start, we are much more used to an economy of wage than one of gift. We are used to paying for things, valuing things by how much they cost and ourselves by how much we are paid. It is not a first instinct to experience the world as a free gift offered by a divine father to his children.

Moreover, those of us who have been followers of Christ for some time may have lost sight of the generosity of the Father. Some traditions in the church are strong on grace as the means by which we enter the Kingdom, but weak on grace as the means by which we go on in the Kingdom. Often, the story is told like this: Jesus gave his life that you might be saved. Now, as an act of gratitude, give your life to him. Romans 12. 1-2 is quoted as Paul's exhortation to do just that.

Many Christians, if they are honest, would say that they look back a little wistfully to the forgiveness and joy they experienced when they first came to Christ. Since then, if truth be told, it has all been drudgery—increasing amounts of responsibility and 'service' at church, trying to cram the extra church-based activities into an already demanding life alongside rearing the kids and earning a crust. Basically, the Christian life just seems to be the 'busier life'. Not that you are resentful of this—after all Christ died for you. It is a worthwhile endeavour to help build the Kingdom. And of course, rest will come one day. But it is certainly not a life of lightness and freedom now.

If you asked most Christians whether they 'serve Christ' as an act of worship, they would say yes. Serving Christ is the appropriate posture toward the King, they say. But did Christ not say that 'The Son of Man did not come to be served but to serve and to give his life as a ransom for many'? Yes, they reply, he did, and he meant that in his earthly life he came to serve. Now, risen and reigning as King, we serve him.

But is this actually true?

I am not so sure. This implies that the posture of God in the incarnation was a one-off, a divine curve ball, rather than the normal trajectory of the posture of God toward his world. It implies that God served for one time only, and after that he got back into his normal position of being served. But that cuts across the heart of the meaning of the incarnation. The incarnation revealed the interior life of the divine community. It revealed the inner nature of God. And that nature, as we see it, is a nature of self-giving. The God who is there is a God who gives himself in love. That is what defines him. The act of service in the incarnation was certainly a unique and specific manifestation of the life and love of God toward his world, but it was not a one-off act. It was consonant with the harmonies of love that continue to play between the persons of God, Father, Son and Spirit.

God continues to serve. Christ continues to serve. The notion that we come to faith through Christ's service and then we turn this orientation round is to misunderstand entirely the radical nature of discipleship and eternal life. The posture of humility in which Peter had to allow the Son of Man to wash his feet is not simply a one-off historical act either for him in AD 33 or for us at our conversion. Rather it postures that being in Christ calls us to adopt each and every moment. That is the essence of being a Christian.

The other way of thinking is so inculcated in us that we rebel against it. How can we allow God to serve us in this way? Is that not the very heart of selfishness that Christ came to change? No. The heart that Jesus came to change is the heart that seeks to make itself safe and self-sufficient in a hostile world, outside a relationship with a divine

Father. Jesus came to change the heart that seeks to continue to earn its wage and pay its way. Jesus seeks to change the heart that remains in control. Jesus seeks to change the heart that is weary, worn out with doing things for other people. The truth is that the life of service can be just as much a strategy to make ourselves safe in the world outside a relationship with a divine Father as the life of rampant licentiousness.

This is the radical, extraordinary and wonderful revelation in the parable Jesus told of the two sons. Neither the first nor the second son where at home with the father. Both were alienated, outside the love of the father. Both had misunderstood the nature of life in the father's house. The first son, driven by the fear of not getting what he wanted, what he thought he needed to be happy, runs away. He cuts the ties to live on his own wits and his Dad's resources. The second son chooses a different strategy. Not believing that there is enough love in the father to stretch to both children and not believing that there is enough produce on the farm for him to have a party for his friends, he works day and night to serve the farm and the father. No wonder he is incandescent when his brother returns and has the fattened calf slaughtered! In his economy his brother is worth nothing.

The parable works on the basis not only of the extraordinary generosity of the father's heart but also of the abundance of the farm. The second son, it implies, had also lived in fear—fear that the farm would not have enough unless it was carefully laboured over, stored, saved and not wasted. He lived as if there was barely enough and worked hard to steward the limited resources. The power of the parable is predicated upon the fact that there was enough on the farm without this. It was unnecessary! The provision was abundant and not restrictive. The parable is not just about the generosity of the divine Father but also his abundance.

The transition required to come into the Kingdom is the transition from believing that we have either the agency to or the responsibility for securing enough for ourselves and others in the world. It is the abandonment of the notion that we are powerful or that we have control in our hands. It is the repenting of the 'adult' posture that plans, organises and produces with a view to being in control and able to cope against all life's eventualities. Much of what goes for Christian discipleship is simply the ecclesiastical version of this. It is the careful stewarding, through our hard work, discipline and commitment, of the limited resources of the church and ourselves in the act of service of the King. All of us who are followers of Christ have lived like this at some time or other. It leaves us exhausted, frustrated and resentful of how much we have done and how little others have done. It leaves us disappointed that God has not blessed our Kingdom initiatives. It leaves us protective of our ministries and hungry for the affirmation of our peers or the pastor. It leaves us cynical of those who come to church but whose lives do not live up to ours.

Living the undefended life is living in the world in a new way. Not in fear, trying to hoard what we can for the future. Not in greed, believing that the Father does not actually know what we need to be happy. Not in exhausting labour trying to make ends meet, fearfully worrying over whether we have saved enough. The undefended life is instead lived in receptive generosity.

Living in the 'day'

The great narrative of such a life is that of the manna and quail provided for the people of Israel in the desert. In this story, God promises to provide enough for his people. They are to collect each morning the strange manna, which has crystallised on the ground. They are to collect what they need for the day—and no more. Some families needed more than others—maybe there were more of them, maybe they had growing teenage lads, maybe they had bigger appetites. That was fine. They did not all collect the same amount but they collected what they needed for the day. They were told not to hoard it or store it; if they did, they found that the next day it had rotted away.

Each day was a daily act of trust. What temptation there must have been to just take a bit more. What if it doesn't come tomorrow? What if I get peckish at about four o'clock? Maybe if I take some more today that will be helpful in case we are ill tomorrow and cannot go out and gather some. No, said God, gather what you need for this day and I will provide again for you tomorrow. Each day there will be a sufficiency.

We find an echo of this in Jesus' language in Matthew 6. There, as we have seen, he ties the life of the child of God to the providential provision of the Father. And it seems that this unit of time—'the day'—is significant on both occasions. Jesus says, 'Do no worry about tomorrow, for tomorrow will worry about itself. Each day has enough trouble of its own'. Clearly in the Exodus story the day lasts for twenty-four hours. In Matthew, I am not sure we should take a day that literally. The intent behind what Jesus is saying is to address the worried and the anxious of the pagan world who live under the fear narrative. He is teaching about how the children of the Kingdom, of the divine Father who is for them, should live. The central mark should be a freedom from this kind of anxiety, and all associated worrying activities, in favour of trusting that the Father, who loves you and knows your need, will provide for you.

Jesus is actually teaching about the abundance of the gift of the world to the child of God. He teaches about the experience of the sparrows. He does so not simply as a contrast (they being of such little importance and we so great) but also because of the similarity. The Father provides for both us and the sparrow. Both are sustained because the Father gives us a world of abundance—rich, plentiful and sufficient for our needs. He does this not as a mechanic who has powered up the engine of the earth, but rather as an involved Father who continually gifts the world to us, to be received and enjoyed.

Birds do stock up for winter. Squirrels do store nuts away. The world, as it is given to us, comes with seasons. There are seasons of growth and seasons of death—summer and winter. The plants and animals of the natural world participate in an ecosystem that involves different activities and rhythms. This is life as 'gift' where one lives according to the 'day' as it is given. Day here implies not simply an amount of time, but a type of time (the Hebrew distinction between time as chronos (length) and time as kairos (moment or kind). We are to receive the day as the kind of time it is.

Each 'day' has trouble enough of its own. Each day has its own work to be done in it. There is a kind of activity that is fitting for the day, for the moment, for the season, for the year, for the stage of one's life. In this 'day' one is called to live in it appropriately. To do the work of today and not the work of tomorrow. We are called to be at peace in the stage and place of life that we have been put. We are called to do so because we have a divine Father who invites us, his children, to receive the 'day', our lives, as gift to us on a moment-by-moment basis.

The pagan lives worrying about 'tomorrow'. He lives in fear; thus he endures the working week by waiting for the weekend and he has all his fun from Saturday to Sunday. He exhaust himself in his twenties and thirties, storing up wealth and influence for himself, perhaps becoming a partner in the firm, in order to retire and 'really start to live' in the tomorrow of his fifties. Or she lives in the disappointment of the relationship she is now in, wishing she had married someone different, always looking over her shoulder at the person she could have been with. They live in the big city, always wishing they were in the country, fleeing in the 4x4 on a Friday evening to the coast where they can really have their life.

All of these lives are living for 'tomorrow'. They are living for a kind of time that they do not actually inhabit now. They are living as if life were not a gift but a commodity to be stored, saved, hoarded and maximised. Living as if life were threat.

The undefended life is the life that is lived in the present. It is lived in the moment and it is lived here and now, in this time and in this space. It is lived with trust that this 'day' has been given to you as a gift and that there is enough in it for you. Jesus is not teaching here that Christians should only ever have enough food in their cupboards for the next twenty-four hours. He is not teaching that Christians should eschew saving up money. He is not teaching financial negligence. Rather, he is saying: 'Do what the Father is inviting you to do at this time of your life.' Do this, and do not do something else instead. Jim Eliot, a young American missionary who lost his life to the cause, properly put it this way: 'Wherever you are, be all there.'

Jesus is inviting us to find our pleasure, our happiness, our enjoyment in the place we are in here and now; for that is where God our Father is and that is where God our Father will meet with us and give us his life. We are to eschew the fantasy that life is over there, or over here, doing this or doing that. That is the way of being in the world in fear. It robs us of all life: when we arrive there we find that it too is empty, for the Father is not present with us.

When my children were young, I struggled as a father. I had accelerated through my childhood and hit adulthood at full tilt. I was always moving onwards, looking ahead, getting to the next stage. I got married young, got ordained young, did my third degree young, and had children young. When my boys arrived, I suddenly hit the time in life when things start to get complicated. Children are messy, and in more ways that one. They disrupt things—patterns of life, concentration, periods of study, holidays, lie-ins, night-times, health, silence and space. Life gets cluttered and I experienced my boys as an obstruction to my trajectory.

I had come to live my life for tomorrow rather than for the 'day' that had been given to me. It brought endless frustration and even anger to be continually held back to the 'day'. I used to look ahead to the boys growing up. Phew, we are now over the toddler stage, now onto the pre-school years. Great, now we are up and running at school, it is only a couple of years before secondary school. Count on....wow, it's just another seven years and they will be gone. And I will be able to have my life back.

Now, of course, I did not always think like this, but it was a narrative never far from my mind. It robbed me of my joy in the present. It started to rob me of my relationship with my boys. It came to a head, in fact, when I became more and more fixated on their futures and whether they would have enough to live on. I became more and more anxious that, somehow, I would have to earn enough, not just for life now, but life in the future—three other families as well (for by now I had a girl as well as two boys!) My mood would go up and down with the prospects of my work and the wider economy. I was tired, distracted, absorbed and irritable, often flying off the handle at them, accusing them of not realising how tough things were.

It was the day, round the kitchen table, when they looked at me and said 'Dad, we don't really like you anymore' that I realised things had gone very wrong. But, despite realising this, I also knew that it seemed beyond my power to change my perception. This root of fear for them gripped me. It was around this same time that I began to write more intently about the call to stillness. Looking back, I was clearly writing of something to which I myself aspired. I was longing for it myself and trying to find how to reach that place. In the end, however, my words were not enough to draw me into that place of stillness. What it took was a catastrophe.

I invested some money badly. By that I mean not only was the investment call wrong and I lost money, but that I should not have done it in the first place. The nature of the investment was bad: it was in a market which served no value in society and which I should have steered a million miles away from. Not only this, but my choice was utterly driven by fear.

To lose a significant chunk of my worldly assets through my fear-driven pathology proved, I believe, to be the only means by which my Father could set me free from the grip of this tap root in my life. I came to realise that this archaeological root of fear had lain underneath not just my behaviour but also the behaviour of other generations in my family. It had held them, like me, in thrall, robbing us all of peace and contentment in life. Like me, it led them to a life of endless disappointment and unfulfilled longing.

Let me tell you that this story is not one that took place in my pre-Christian days. This is recent. I was a published author and ordained minister for more than ten years. I have been teaching how to live an undefended life for almost a decade. I tell you this to give you hope and realism. It takes a long time for our deep pathologies to be worked up to the surface. And they do not all get dealt with in one go. This was not the first major bit of archaeological groundwork the Father had done for me, nor will it be the last. God can only work with us bit by bit. Or perhaps he graciously allows us to retain some of the knots in the tangle of our fabric, knowing that were he to pull all of them out in one go the entire garment would collapse.

Our Father is patient and tender with us and does the work that is needed in the season we are in. My divine Father was at work releasing me from the fear that prevented me stepping into my fatherhood. He was giving me back the 'day' of my children. I receive that day as a gift and choose to live in it. I choose to give space and time, here and now, to the gifts around me, at the cost of my career, my writing or my work. I choose not to worry about what we shall wear, or how we shall live 'tomorrow'. For tomorrow will take care of itself. I choose to live in 'this day' and to be the person the Father is inviting me to be in 'this day'.

I have written elsewhere of the timing of God in relation to leaders. More often than not, God's sense of time is not our sense of time. We continue to work in an economy of chronos, seeking to extract what we need or can from the unit of twenty-four hours that is in front of us. This is to live in the narrative of fear. Instead, God invites us to step into the life of the Spirit, whereby he promises life in 'this day'. He invites us to share this day with him and to join in with what he is doing here and now. It is not ours to know what moments in our life will be of significance or of lasting value. All we are called to do is to respond to the call of the moment, to be fully present and available. What end that will have is something we can leave up to Another.

Relinquishing control but taking responsibility

The undefended life is a life in which we take responsibility but relinquish control. The fear narrative tends to reverse these postures. Most people live their lives trying to take as much control as they can and abandon as much responsibility as possible. They feel reassured when their bank balance is plump, their holidays are planned, their children's schooling laid out and their career path clear. This gives them a sense of control. 'The future is mapped out. I am secure. Nothing can come along and trip me up.' At the same time, they often do their best to shirk responsibilities for their choices. They close their eyes to the origins of the clothing they are buying at absurdly cheap prices or the provenance of the meat they put on their plates. They neglect their responsibility to their local community as they uproot themselves once again in order to buy property in another up-and-coming area. They abdicate responsibility for anyone other than themselves on their way to work each day, plugged into their iPod or Blackberry, sweeping past the toiling mother carrying her buggy up the stairs in the tube station or simply failing ever to learn the name of the receptionist on the front desk.

The undefended life is a life in which we relinquish control but take up our responsibilities. One of the chief things I am responsible for is my life. I cannot simply say, 'I am Simon Walker. These are my strengths. These are my weaknesses. Take it or leave it. I can't change me.' That is an abdication of responsibility. As I have said, nothing in my life—my character, my personality—is immune from the ways I have sought to make myself safe in this world. All of me is involved and complicit in that strategic act. And God will not tolerate me simply putting parts of me out of his reach. That denies my personal responsibility.

The undefended life is a life of continual openness to the penetrating reach of God. It is never fully settled. It never reaches a point where it is content, at ease, fully OK. It is particularly sensitive to the iterated and hardened patterns of behaviour that have not changed in many years or even many decades. It does not settle for a coping strategy, for a bit of scaffolding to limit the damage. It continues to invite God to re-weave the most tangled, knotted and historic parts of our selves. Thus, someone living an undefended life holds conclusions lightly. Everything they know, everything they hold is theirs, not as a permanent, fixed security but rather as a provisional gift of God for the moment, for the day. It may be that another day will come in which we will be invited to relinquish control of that with which we have become too familiar — be it a job, role, position, ability, reputation or whatever.

Taking risks

The undefended life is essentially one of absurd risks. I suggested earlier that the basic characteristic of conversion is not moral reform, but risk. Faith is not a form of piety but a ludicrous risk comprising the abandonment of that which has made us safe up to this point in favour of trusting that our divine Father will make us safe. All of the undefended life, therefore, involves small and incremental acts of risk-taking. I am reminded of my wife who, just this week, took the risk of offering herself for a job. For her, the risk of rejection or failing would normally have meant she would not do such a thing. It also makes her an exceptional practitioner at her job. But that excellence is part of the strategy she uses to defend herself. To abandon that must therefore involve her running the risk of failing, of being judged and found to be wanting. God is not interested in my wife as a utility to do a job with excellence; he is interested in her as a daughter of his in whose heart he wants to put more of his love. My wife, like any one of us, can only experience more of the love of the Father when she abandons the strategies she has used to make herself safe in favour of experiencing his affection for her in each and every moment.

It is easy to think that risk-taking always involves doing something new and 'out there'. My wife took this kind of risk, but there are other kinds of risks as well. Sometimes it is more risky to stick with the same activity that we have been doing up to the present moment. There is a kind of pathology in which fear is assuaged by endless change and revision.

Imagine a brother and sister called Wilf and Wilma. Wilma is a little older than Wilf and she has always been quick to give an answer. The answers were not always right, mind you, but, nevertheless, at school she found that putting her hand up first often got her more attention than sitting quietly and waiting. Wilma would often be the first child to suggest a new game in the playground; if there was a new craze she generally got into it first; if a new kid came into class she was usually the first to welcome them. If you drew a line of the typical learning curve, you would see that Wilma's curve went up a little bit faster than those of most other children. By the time it got to the top, she was no better than other people at her subjects but early on, at the start of the curve, she was slightly ahead of the game.

Wilf, on the other hand, learned that it was hard to 'out-speak' his sister. It was difficult to get in first because she was talkative and always had something to suggest. So he did not try very hard to develop those skills. Instead, he discovered that if he kept at the same activity for long enough then sooner or later his sister would give up. 'I'm bored', she would say. He knew that if he kept going at this point then he would be able to do the activity better than her. And that was what made him feel successful and also what got him the praise of teachers.

So Wilma developed the characteristic of being a quick initiator and Will the characteristic of 'stickability'. Here is the question: which one of the two, Wilf or Wilma, is the biggest risk taker?

The answer is, of course, neither. They were both risk averse. Wilf is risk averse in a way that we recognise today. He did not like change. Change for him meant that he had to start again at the bottom of the learning curve. Down there he was always behind others for a bit and so he felt vulnerable. He felt comfortable when things remained the same for some time. He was risk averse.

But Wilma was also risk averse. For her, risk was found at the top of the learning curve. Here, she lost her competitive advantage over the other children. At this point, her strategy—in order to make herself safe again in the world, to secure attention and success over others around her—was to initiate a new activity. In other words, she went back to the beginning of the learning curve. Wilma made herself safe by changing things. It was stability that was risky for her.

Risk is not about doing new things; it is about doing the one thing that is not safe for us. For me, that will be different from what it is for you. What looks mad and risky to you may be the safest thing in the world for me. There is a particular 'spiritual guise' to this experience of risk. I was helping a Christian leader to explore his patterns of defended behaviour. During the session on Wilf and Wilma, it was as if a light bulb went on for him. He told me how, during his Christian life, he had always interpreted a sense of anxiety or disquiet inside himself as confirmation from the Spirit that this course of action was not the right one. A spirituality that encourages us to be led by the Spirit might easily suggest that a sense of peace is a confirmation that 'God is in this' and that uncertainty and fear are signs that we might have gone the wrong way.

My friend suddenly realised that his own internal strategies, which were very like those of Wilf, were the alarm calls going off inside him when things became too risky. Far from joining in with the movements of God he was resisting them, choosing to stay safe in his own iterated psychological strategies. The movements of the Spirit would precisely involve unsettling those settled areas.

On the other hand, some Christian traditions value and prize continual change in the way they offer corporate worship. They like to be inventing new things, singing new songs and starting new kinds of services. Sometimes they gloss this with the language of 'listening to the Spirit' or 'moving with the Spirit'. Now, the Spirit of God is always opening up the world from its closed, fearful structures and strategies. But, paradoxically, this can involve His leading us to remain content with what we are currently doing rather that moving on to a new thing. The breath of the Spirit may just, from time to time, call us to old forms of worship and tradition. That same Spirit may call parts of the church that have become wedded to those same forms of worship to relinquish their control of them. God calls us neither to endless change nor fixed stability, but rather to a gracious movement in time, in pace, with his Spirit.

Freedom

Jesus says that 'If the Son sets you free, you will be free indeed.' This freedom, we imagine, is much more than the simple, though wonderful, freedom from the guilt and condemnation ensuing from a future judgement. I want to suggest at least five different freedoms which are ours as we abandon the fear narrative in favour of the undefended life in the Spirit.

Freedom to feel

As we experience the intimate attachment of the divine Father, so our own emotional needs are met. They may be met directly through an intimate personal encounter, or they may be met through the nourishing, nurturing gift of 'the day' as God our Father gives it to us. Either way, we receive the gift of his emotional provision for us in such a way that our deep emotional deficits may be gradually resolved in Him. As a result of this, we become more and more able to 'feel for others'—to hold other people's feelings and to have the space for deep and appropriate emotional attention.

If our own emotional needs are not met, then our responses to another person's emotions will always be clouded; we may be intolerant because no-one was patient with us. We may be bitter because we were never recognised. We may be fearful toward another person's story of risk because we ourselves would be frightened in such circumstances. Our ability to be available for the other is dependent on the degree to which our own emotional needs are met. If I am to have 'space for your feelings', someone else must first have had 'space for my feelings'. Otherwise, there is no room for any more emotions.

The person living the undefended life does not jump in with a solution for your problems straight away. They do not always share their own similar experiences (a way of resolving their own unfinished emotional business). They do not always tell you that, despite the bleakness of your situation, 'God is teaching you things' or 'God will heal in the end'. They can live with situations which have no apparent resolution; and, in so doing, they offer you the gift of an accepting and hospitable space where you are welcome to stay 'as you are' rather than being led on at their pace.

Freedom to focus

I devote a lot of my attention and energy to making myself safe in the world. As a result, I am often unable to focus on what actually needs to be done. I may look as if I am paying you attention but, in fact, I may be working out what I need to do to look clever or appear competent, in control or likeable. The person living an undefended life is not so preoccupied. They do not stare over your shoulder at the party, thinking about who they are going to talk to next. They do not glance endlessly at their watch. They do not forget important things that you have entrusted to them. Instead, they are attentive and focused. You feel heard when you have been with them.

At the same time, they also have clarity of thought and insight because they are able to attend to all the relevant data. Unlike most people, who do their best to overlook data which is uncomfortable, the person who is undefended has no such agenda. They do not need a particular outcome from your conversation or out of the work. Thus they can be even-handed and open-minded. They can welcome all relevant parties to the table. In this way, the person who is undefended has a more efficient and effective mind than the defended person.

Freedom to fail

We are often told these days that there is no such thing as failure. Instead, failures are really learning opportunities. Much of the time this may be right. We can learn from any experience. However, if we take that axiom as a means of avoiding the truth of loss, grief, disappointment or rejection, then we are simply finding another way to defend ourselves from pain. The truth is that there will be times in our lives when we fail—genuinely fail. We may fail an exam. We may fail to get a job. We may fail to protect a life. We may fail to overcome an illness. We may fail to win the approval of people that matter. We may fail to lead someone to Christ. These experiences cannot be simply glossed as learning opportunities. The emotions of pain, sadness, confusion, shame and grief are very real. Not only this, but we must also do the good work of incorporating these difficult stories into the narrative of our life.

If we are defended, the stories without a happy ending or an upbeat note are problematic. Hence, some try to invent a happy ending or deny the pain that they have caused. But, to the person who is undefended, no loss is so devastating as to threaten their security or identity. They know who they are as a child of their divine Father, and nothing can separate them from this identity. Indeed, it seems that God often allows us experience failure in order that we might incorporate this loss into our story. God allowed Jacob, Moses, Joseph, Samson and Paul, to name but a few, to experience significant failures and losses and to learn to live with the disability it brought in order that they might rely more fully on His grace. It seems that, particularly for those who are trusted with significant authority, some 'thorn' that renders them weak serves as an antidote to the threat of believing in their own success and power.

Freedom to forgive

Forgiveness is difficult to comprehend from the perspective of the guilt narrative. We can perhaps forgive someone because we know that we have been forgiven. We can perhaps forgive someone if we believe that one day they will face judgement for their actions. But those who have forgiven in the most remarkable and extraordinary ways often speak with a certain urgency about the need to forgive. They maintain that forgiveness has been the only way that they can find life. More than that, they report that their lives would have been damaged if they had not forgiven.

I think that such people exemplify, perhaps more powerfully than in any other human choice, the life that is ours when we are redeemed from the fear narrative. To choose retribution or revenge, or simply to harbour anger, is, as I have said, to maintain a posture of hostility toward another. We allow their act of violence to continue to have power over us; it robs us of peace. This power perpetuates the story of an unsafe world in which the predominant posture of one to another is that of threat. This power puts hostility in the centre once again. As such, I believe—if I may take the risk of speaking for them—such forgiving people choose to reject the fear narrative and all its destructive power.

We see in them someone who has been able to lay down aggression and hostility. Almost always, people who show extraordinary forgiveness have chosen to become aware of the background of the perpetrators. They have chosen to see them not simply as an agent of pain, but also as a victim of pain—as someone who needs help and, most of all, freedom from the fearful, loveless world in which they have come to live. The act of forgiveness reverses the spirals of fear in the world, breeding trust and healing pain. It involves the almost unimaginable choice to relinquish the story of revenge which can soothe the terrible pain of the sufferer in favour of reaching for a source of soothing that is yet more powerful. That human beings forgive is, for me, the greatest testimony to the fact that life is found in being undefended rather than defended.

Freedom to fight

This may sound contradictory after what I said in the previous section about forgiveness, but I believe that both the freedom to forgive and the freedom to fight are available to the undefended person. When people sometimes hear the term 'undefended life' for the first time, they understand it to mean being vulnerable or even being a kind of doormat, allowing others to walk all over them. The term 'undefended', at face value, does seem to imply not stopping people doing things to you. However, I have explained above that being undefended means laying down one's own defences in favour of allowing God your Father to defend you. In this, to become undefended may, for some people, involve acts of self-protection and assertion in the face of inappropriate intrusion of hostility.

Earlier in this book I told the story of the woman who had been bleeding for many years. I believe Jesus 'defended her' to the crowd when he said 'Woman, go in peace'. I believe this was a command to that community to stop denying her the privileges of full society. I believe it was an assertion of her boundaries, of her space in the world, of the legitimate status of a daughter of God. To be undefended for her was, in fact, to choose to abandon the old, diminished view of herself. It meant, from that day onwards, walking tall, head held high, maintaining eye contact and speaking in an audible voice.

Thus, the undefended narrative can quite easily incorporate acts which protect and dignify those who society has judged and dismissed. Once again, think of the woman caught in adultery who was brought to Jesus. Rather than judging her, he protected her from the hostility of her accusers. More than this, Jesus was capable of acts of strength, and even violence and aggression in his own 'undefendedness'. When he cast out the demons, confronted Satan and flung over the tables of the moneychangers in the temple, Jesus was no door mat. He was fighting against that which was abusing and destroying something precious and sacred. Jesus was able to do such a thing because he was not ruled by fear. He was not subject to an instinct of self-protection. Instead, he was available to serve in the situation as it was appropriate.

Few of us relish confrontation. In some parts of the world, to confront or to upset the apple cart is a cardinal sin. This 'virtue' has often been enshrined in norms of church behaviour. The church becomes a place where the members are endlessly nice to each other. Indeed, for many, the experience of relationships with others in church circles never gets beyond a kind of friendly banality. 'Home Groups' can be an archetypal form of such Christian insipidness and fear. Week by week, small groups of church members gather in each others' homes to drink coffee and study some scripture together. Despite having had hours of contact time, members may and often do conceal rather than disclose. Individuals trot out the same story of their selves and their problems. The same prayers are repeated for the personal sagas which the group members are struggling with—a difficult marriage, a son who has broken ties with his parents or an unfair boss. Sympathy is offered and tolerance shown.

The members lack the wisdom, the will and the courage to create an environment that will press any further into the reality of the situation. What of the depths of pain that a person must be feeling! What of the sense of fear or anger they must be struggling with. What of their anger toward God? In the half-hour prayer time, such emotional topographies are skated over with the briefest of glimpses, just as tourists in the tour bus notice a few highlights in the landscape from a distance and through the window, without ever taking the time, or the risk, to stop and explore. Such emotional tourism may only serve to leave that individual unknown and unheard. Nor does it help that person take responsibility for their actions. Their part is often tacitly condoned. (Yet privately some in the group may not be surprised that the son of the repressive and frankly judgmental mother wants no further contact with her. Privately, others may see a degree of unchallenged myopia and immaturity in the husband whose wife has become closed to him.)

The stitchwork in peoples' lives requires far deeper and more careful scrutiny if any real change is to take place. But such work is beyond the intent and perhaps the skill of that community. You might respond that such deep dysfunctions lie in the domain of the professional marriage counsellor and therapist. Yes, in this day and age, they do. But those professions exist in the main because our society at large has lost the ability and wisdom to listen, hear and hold the lives of one another in any great depth. Most people live entirely untended lives in which they scurry around an array of external obligations, distracting themselves from the sorrow or emptiness within.

As our range of diverting technologies has increased, so we have found more and more ways to soothe ourselves and distract ourselves from any proper introspection. Our own emotional and social literacy is so limited and immature that we reduce conversation to mere information gathering. We have substituted human encounter with ever-growing technological means of 'touching each other' without risk of commitment, discipline, honesty and depth. When we do encounter each other in person, our attempts at forming intimacies are inevitably clumsy, inappropriate and premature. Perhaps never before has a civilisation existed that is so unable to navigate the waters of human encounter carefully and tenderly. We cannot ask too much of the church, perhaps, in such times, given the general blindness in which we all drift.

Sometimes, too, the watching world misunderstands Christian virtue as a kind of endless tolerance and acceptance without boundary. The popular myth is that Christian behaviour should be perpetually forgiving and never judging. The church is depicted as intolerant, hostile and judgmental when it discriminates between different forms of behaviour on moral grounds. The church is seen as cruel when it excludes one of its members. Sadly, some of these experiences do in fact reflect small-mindedness or lack of grace in the church. However, the act of judging is in itself not invalid for the follower of Christ. Jesus judged in order to protect what was sacred or vulnerable and the undefended life has the courage to do likewise.

What if church really was the space in which we felt truly safe enough to be undefended? What if that was the central, transformational characteristic of this community? Not sound beliefs, and not even social action, but pure safety. 'Come to me all who are heavy laden and I will give you rest.' Is that what the Gospel, the Good News, actually is about?

Chapter 8

Stillness and Movement

"Action which does not derive from stillness is mere technique and diminishes those acted upon."

Maggie Ross

Jesus was free enough to risk his life. He was free enough to act boldly, decisively in confrontation, to protect that which was sacred. It was not the only strategy he chose to use but it was the one that was right at that moment in time. It was right because Jesus, as we need now to consider, lived his life in a state of attentiveness to the movements of the Father and a freedom to join in with them.

The central posture of the undefended life is one of both concurrent stillness and movement. John's Gospel opens up more deeply than any other part of the bible the interior life of the community of God. John narrates the words of Jesus, the divine Son, as he articulates how he experiences the relationship with his Father and with the Spirit. One of the most important disclosures Jesus makes about this reality is in John 5. 19: 'The Son...can only do what he sees his Father doing, because whatever the Father does the Son also does. For the Father loves the Son and shows him all that he does.'

If there is one thing I would have the reader take away from this book, it is the significance of these lines. It is upon this that everything I have written hangs. Jesus is describing his posture in the world in relation to the Father. He says that everything he does—every single thing—he does because he has seen his Father doing it. Jesus does not act autonomously. Jesus moves always and only in time, in pace, in space, with the movements of his Father. Indeed, the defining attribute of the intimacy of Father and Son is that the Father shows the Son everything he does. He discloses himself fully to be known by the Son. There is no separation.

Eternal life is to know God as Jesus makes him known. Eternal life is to experience this quality of intimacy and disclosure of the Father to his sons and daughters. This dynamic has two aspects to it. The first is stillness. Jesus is always still enough, at every moment, to detect the movements of the Father in that space. He has a quality of attention, of listening, such that he is aware of the movements of the Father on a momentary basis.

Now, consider this. In most moments your mind, if it is anything like mine, is a continual stream of thoughts, ideas, feelings and images, which jump in and out of it. At times, your mind is fixated, preoccupied with some task, requiring all concentration; you block out every other noise, not noticing what is going on around you. At other times, your mind is vacant, drifting aimlessly, being caught like a leaf on the breeze, unfocused. At times, your mind is busy, searching for the right thing to say or do; in the midst of the conversation with your boss, your neighbour or the shop owner, you are distracted, thinking of something else, working out what to say in response, trying to engineer the conversation to go where you want it to go. You feel frustration, irritation or fear (Oh, just hurry up! Let me speak! No, you're wrong! I have the answer to this! Oh, please don't tell me that! What does she mean? I hope I don't sound stupid. I must avoid getting found out here.)

Your mind, if it is like mine, is endlessly full—planning, scripting, avoiding, solving, fretting, organising and drifting. Now, compare this again to Jesus. 'The Son can only do what he sees his Father in heaven doing.' Jesus' mind was not like my mind. His mind was, he tells us, always in a posture of stillness and attention to the movements of the Father. He had space to notice what his Father was doing. It was not that at the beginning of the day, during his prayer time, his Father downloaded the plan for the day or the week to him and he executed it. No, this was experience revealed in every moment that he watched and listened to the Father.

Why is my mind so full and cluttered? The answer is that I am endlessly making strategies for ways to make myself safe. Analyse your thoughts for a moment. If you are honest there is a sub-text to most of what you are thinking. You do not always think about the activity at hand, but rather a host of other peripheral thoughts. I am preparing dinner, but instead of paying attention to cutting the vegetables and the children's conversation I am caught up in plans for the meeting tomorrow. I am clock-watching trying to get it all done by 6:00pm. I am stewing over the slight at work that day. In other words, I am busy reassuring myself that my plans and strategies for life are working. I am doing mental and emotional housework, tidying round my little internal rooms to see what has got disordered that day, dusting things down, putting them back straight and making mental notes not to allow this or that person to come in again. I am soothing myself, staying in control and feeling OK.

If I pray, it is the prayer that begs God to come and join me in this activity, to smooth over some bumps, to ease the problems and rifts or to give me strength to keep going. Prayer is my means of getting God to do the housework with me.

Look again at what Jesus says: 'The Son can only do what he sees his Father in heaven doing, because whatever the Father does the Son also does.' This sounds very different from the way I experience the Father. Jesus is not co-opting God to join him in his mental planning and business. Jesus is seeking to be still and quiet enough in himself, to notice what the Father is doing, so that he can join in with him. Why does he do that? Apparently it is because the very act of participating in the movements of the Father is what characterises their love. 'For the Father loves the Son and shows him all he does.' Apparently, the divine life is, and only is, the joining in with the movements of the Father as the Son.

Are we missing out on eternal life in all the little moments because we allow ourselves to be so preoccupied with the mental and emotional scripts that run endlessly round our heads? Is it possible that eternal life is available to us in each and every moment but that most of the time we choose to ignore it, instead staying planted in our own, self-referential world?

More than being quiet

Now, you might hear this as a call to quietism. This may sound like a life which is withdrawn from the rush of the world into a place of quiet. But, if you look again at what Jesus says, we see that this is not the case. 'My Father is always at his work', Jesus says a few verses earlier. So, Jesus, too, who does only what he sees his Father in heaven doing, is always joining in the work of God. Apparently, this posture involves action. It is a kind of stillness, of attentiveness, which then becomes freely available to join in with the action (the movement) of the Father. These two postures, stillness and action, are not consecutive: they are concurrent. Within the movement of the Son, there is always a part of him which is still. There is a way of being in the world which is always at rest.

And we can rest because God has adopted us as his children. God the Father draws us into a space in which we experience ourselves as his children. In this space we are freed from the fear narrative by our intimate encounter with God's love. This love is eternal life. It is always the place where we come home. It is a place where we can rest and be still. In this place we receive the love of the Father. We are children of God in each and every moment. But in this place, we find ourselves caught up in the movements of the Father. We are invited to participate with Him in the world. Thus, our actions are a responsive movement of flow in love, in time and pace with the Father, through the Spirit.

T. S. Eliot explores this paradox of movement and stillness in his poems 'The Four Quartets'. He suggests this as 'the still point of the turning world' which is 'neither arrest nor fixity, neither from nor towards'.[2] Later, he invites us into the image of a divine dance in which we are to move in measure like a dancer. From this we might conceive that the movements themselves are God, an interpenetrating dance of Father, Son and Spirit in which we are invited to participate. Lest we might think of this dance as just one way of being in the world, or experiencing life, he asserts that 'there is only the dance'.[3] In other words, the nature of the world is constituted in movement, in the circulating relations of the divine persons in community. This is life. Life is not found outside this space, nor is it found in fixity within this space. It is within the dance that we exist because God exists only in the dance.

Here we find ourselves drawn deeply into a theological notion of God as existing (or better subsisting) not as three independent persons but as a mutually indwelling community in which the Father, Son and Spirit endlessly interpenetrate each other in movements of self-giving, self-disclosing and receiving. The relations of the triune God are opened up to us and in them we find life. It is not wrong to say, therefore, that God in his eternal nature is undefended. By this we mean that God's nature is constituted by his openness and giving to another. God in himself does not conceal or hide himself in fear. Nor is God territorial or defensive. Nor is it possible for the persons of God to exist autonomously, outside the interpenetrating relations with the

---

2   In T. S. Eliot, Collected Poems, 1909-1962 (London: Faber and Faber, 2002).

3   Ibid.

Other. The persons of God are not self-referential; they do not find life on their own terms, within their own personal resources.

We find ourselves approaching the deep truth that the undefended life comes to us not as an idea but as the reality of God, as He is in himself. To adapt Eliot's words, we must live the undefended life, because there is 'only the undefended life'. The God who is, is vulnerable and undefended within himself.

Chapter 9

The God who is Undefended

"God is not solitude, but perfect communion."

Benedict XVI

It is not possible to write a book about the undefended life without enquiring about the 'undefendedness' of God. Our lives flows from the life that is within God and, therefore, if this characteristic is to be properly human then it is so only because it is first properly of God.

The narrative of God's self-disclosure in the bible is not without violence. I have offered some reflection on the dynamic of aggression as part of a posture of undefendedness when it comes to the protection of that which is vulnerable and sacred. I do not wish to attempt a more thorough exegesis of the stories in the bible of a God who acts, and indeed calls others to act, with violence. What I do say is that if those stories are to find legitimacy as acts of the divine then they must do so on the basis of the kind of account I am offering. In other words, they must be able to be seen as movements by God to protect that which is sacred and vulnerable from forces, people, societies and religious traditions that would otherwise desecrate or destroy them.

I am willing to sit under such a hermeneutical paradigm because it seems overwhelmingly clear that the arc of the movements of God towards his world is decisively undefended rather than defended. We can see this in the narrative of God's relationship to the Jews in the bible. He commits himself to a posture of forgiveness and acceptance of these people as a continuing, future orientation (the covenant) such that their religion involves the abandoning of the rituals and totems that secure the favour of the capricious gods, in favour of trusting that their God is 'for them'. The arc of the revelation of YHWH is that he is trustworthy and will trust his people. Moreover, he adopts this posture in the face of humankind's rejection of this basic posture in Genesis 3. God's movement is redemptive of a prior rejection and therefore involves forgiveness, generosity, mercy, patience and love as its very core threads.

We find that this arc of undefended love touches the ground of this fallen world most vulnerably in the act of the incarnation. God discloses himself not merely through word, nor through action, but through 'becoming one of us'. God enters in. This act of incarnation, Paul contends, is fundamentally an act of kenosis, or self-emptying. In Philippians 2, he quotes a Christian hymn of the time:

> *Jesus...who being in very nature God*
> *Did not consider equality with*
> *God something to be grasped,*
> *But made himself nothing,*
> *Taking the very nature of a servant*
> *Being made in human likeness.*
> *And being found in appearance as a man*
> He humbled himself and became obedient to death
>
> *—even death on a cross.*   (Philippians 2. 5-8)

In the Incarnation, God lays down his power. The divine Son, who is equal to God and made of the same nature of God, sets aside his power, his freedom and his non-contingency and chooses willingly to submit himself to a kind of contingent, limited existence. Such an act can be described in no other terms than as the archetypal movement of undefendedness.[4]

4   Moltmann and Fiddes explore the notion of risk in the incarnation and crucifixion and are the chief architects of a version of God's suffering that cannot leave a part of him immune and safeguarded from the act of death

In the Incarnation God also risks himself. Many Christians are tempted to see Jesus' life, death and resurrection as a set-piece of theatre in which the ending is a foregone conclusion. The script has already been written and the play performed in the heavenly realms. God the Father knows the outcome; it is simply that the acts must be performed in history to make it effective. This, however, is to misunderstand the nature of God and his own vulnerability.

Whilst God calls his world, and specifically his people, to a posture of trust in him, he has never compelled their subordination to this invitation. The world that God brings into being is not some mechanism that he winds up. Nor is it some doll that he manipulates. In the act of the creation, God risks, making a world which is genuinely 'other' from himself.

A Vulnerable God

This notion of God risking himself is difficult for many to comprehend because of the mental image of divinity that we have in our imaginations. Most people, if they were to try to conceive of it as an image, would imagine the relationship between God and the world something like this: God is there and has always been there. He is vast and huge. He chooses to create a world; we see this world as a separate object from God. It sits alongside him and the entire universe is minute next to the vastness of God, like a beach ball in his hand. God gives the world a degree of choice and freedom. When things go wrong in the world God intervenes, squeezing himself into its tiny parameters, to set things right. This act has re-structured the inner workings of the world such that those within it can now choose to relate properly again to the God who is there, outside the creation. God in Christ has now

itself. See the recommended reading for Jurgen Moltmann's *Theology of Hope* (1967), *The Crucified God* (1974), *The Future of Creation* (1979) and *The Trinity and the Kingdom of God* (1981); and also Paul Fiddes' *The Creative Suffering of God* (1988).

returned to his realm outside the world and watches from on high, influencing events by his Spirit. One day, God will wrap the world up. The earthly creation destroyed, God will translate (resurrect) those who turned back to him freely into a non-earthly state in which they can live forever with him in his realm (heaven).

There are variations on this theme but this, essentially, is the cosmology that many Western Christians understand and live within. In such an image, it is difficult to comprehend the nature of the risk of God in the incarnation. God risks, yes, in squeezing into the world. He is subject to the parameters of the world for the period of time he is in it. But, they assert, because God is before and after the existence of the world and because he always exists, Christ, who for a time squeezes into the world, is known by God to survive the experience and return to the heavenly realm. The outcome of the incarnation is known prior to the event. That is why, they say, God can predict it in the prophecies made in the scriptures. Jesus was living out the course of events that were inevitably going to play out. Somewhere, in this, there is mystery that mankind is still free and people choose to play the roles that they do. God cannot be blamed for what we did to Christ because we were genuinely responsible. They accept that we cannot understand how we could be responsible and that God is also pre-existing and post-existing; but most of us are happy to accept we have come to the boundary of our limited understanding and tolerate this paradox as mystery.

Some theologians, however, have argued that such a picture fails adequately to account for the death of Christ. They argue that, if God always knew Christ would survive—that he was, in some sense, still in existence in the heavenly realms outside time—then Jesus cannot be said to have genuinely suffered.[5] Moreover, they argue that God's own experience of suffering in such an account is insufficient for him to truly 'know' what it is to be human. After all, human beings do not suffer knowing the outcome. We struggle with cancer or disability

---

5   Ibid.

without confidence of wha will happen to us in the end. If God is to truly 'know' this kind of life then he must also relinquish foreknowledge.

They point out that the death of Christ in our place is predicated upon the appropriate equivalence of one for another. If Jesus is not actually fully like us then he cannot die our death. He cannot die for us. God cannot say that 'one of us' has been punished.[6] Some also point out that we cannot really pray to God unless he has suffered with us, for prayer is predicated on the experience that God has had of our lives. God's empathy and his compassion is dependent upon his having truly known what it is to be so vulnerable.

There are, then, a host of problems in accepting this kind of view of the world and God. It seems like it has missed something. It is almost as if, like Newtonian mechanics, it can offer a coherent account of the world but it is not an account which is actually adequate. Newtonian laws of physics are helpful to us because they seem to work on a daily basis. However, physicists tell us that they are not actually a proper description of the physical world. They work because they get close enough for the most part. However, in their entirety they misunderstand the nature of things. Thus all their conclusions are out, just a bit. In the main, most of us to do not notice the gap but, scientifically, we are accepting an entirely erroneous account the world.

This kind of theology seems rather like that. By and large, it works for us; and for this reason we tolerate it. Yes, we can accept that it has flaws when pushed to its philosoph ical limits, but does that matter? I have come to believe that it does matter. It matters because how we answer this question determines how we live in this world. And most of us are in agreement that we urgently need to find another way of doing that.

---

6   Frances Young, from her own personal experience, argues for the necessity of God fully to give up power if he is to be truly available to us. See Face to Face, A Narrative Essay in the Theology of Suffering (1980).

How Can God be Vulnerable?

Western thought owes its origins to classical Greek philosophy. I have already depicted the view of time and timelessness that the Greeks, through Plato, understood. This led the Greeks to assume that absolute being—in other words, true reality—was outside time. It existed in an ideal state, as a type or form. God, if he was to be God, must then also be conceived as outside time—the source from which all types, forms or ideals are derived. Reality is the poor shadow of the ideal that is within God.

When the church came to reflect on the nature of the God, as it was revealed in the bible in the second and third centuries, this view of reality coloured her thinking. God is depicted as one God, but three persons: Father, Son and Spirit. God the Father is the ideal of father; God the Son, the ideal son; God the Spirit, the ideal spirit. Each person of the trinity represents the ideal forms of these human realities. Yet, God is not plural; the entire scriptures make plain that there is one God—God is one. The three persons of the trinity are not three gods vying with each other. They are not three independent beings: they are one being. But how can this be? How can three separate persons be actually one being?

This led the church into a history of theological conundrums. Some theologians argued that the three persons of God are three states in which God exists. Just as water can be in three states (solid, liquid and gas) so God can be in three states (Father, Son and Spirit). The problem with this is that it seems to diminish the personhood of each. Others suggested that God the Father, Son and Spirit are related as a person and their words and their breath are related. So, the Father speaks his word (John refers to Jesus in the prologue of his Gospel as logos, the 'word of God'), through his breath (Spirit, which in Greek and Hebrew is the same word as breath). Thus we can say that God is one, but comes to us in different forms, each of which represents the fullness of God. This seems a better way of approaching the co-relations of God, Father, Son and Spirit, but it still leaves us with an overly functional and singular notion which de-prioritises the Son and the Spirit. After all, my words and my breath come from my mind (the Father in this image), which controls them.

Others suggested that God is, in himself, one but that he is able to express himself into the created world as three. All three of the persons are fully God; they have the essence of God in them, but they represent different and particular aspects of God's full nature. Thus, the Son is fully God. He has the divine nature in him in heaven. But God has a different form when clothed in history—in the flesh as Jesus. Thus, Jesus can say that he is both fully God and fully man at the same time. However, this distinction between the God who is transcendent and separate from this world and time, and the God who is immanent and involved, undermines the vulnerability of God as I have already suggested. Jesus on the cross does not fully die, and God does not suffer in the way that we would because his transcendent essence is separate from this event.

All of these are an attempt to maintain the divinity of God in his essence. They assume that divinity is itself 'an ideal or perfection' a kind of characteristic which must be in the divine and all three persons of the divine. This leads to attempts to preserve the deity of each member of the trinity whilst asserting their distinctiveness and without resulting in three gods.

What lies at the root of these 'gaps', then, is not the theology of God per se but rather a philosophical understanding of reality as 'ideal / type / form / essence'. We find this difficult to perceive because of the intellectual and cultural waters in which we have been swimming for two millennia. But, let us stretch our imaginations. Imagine, for a moment, that there is no such thing as the essence of God, in the sense that it might be distilled. Imagine that the essence of God, if we are to use that term at all, is not found in some substance, or quality, or set of characteristics which can be described, but is rather constituted by a kind of relating.

Relationship as the Essence of Vulnerability

Imagine that the 'essence' of God is the mutual, self-giving disclosure that flows perpetually between the persons of the community of God. Imagine that God's nature is not found within each of the persons but between them, but that God is the quality of trust, of openness, of love that flows between them. Imagine that the divine being is an endless event of love, of movements in and through each other, in which each person defers to the other and, in the same gesture, receives the gift from and of the other. Imagine that the persons of the community of God exist because of the particular character of the gift they give to the others.

The Son is the Son because he is known by the Father; the Son is the Son because he gives himself to the Father in submission, in affection, in receiving his love and following in time, in space, with him. The Father is the Father because he loves the Son and discloses all that he does to him. The Father is the Father because he does not conceal or hold back but opens himself, his heart, his passion, his movements, his gestures and acts to the Son, such that he never acts independently or alone. The Spirit is the Spirit because he perpetually moves out from the Father, bearing his love and provoking the Father and the Son outwards to include the Other (where the Other is that which is not God and thus includes the creation and all that is in it). The Spirit is the Spirit because he both bears the word of the Son, carrying the presence of the Son to the Father and yet, at the same time, disrupts the circularity of the reference of Father to Son, carrying the scent of this relationship further and wider. The Spirit is the Spirit because he draws the Other that is outside the Father and Son into relationship with the Father and Son, into their midst.

Imagine that the divine nature is not found in any one of the persons of the triune community, nor in all of them as some essence of their being, but rather through their corporate, communal interpenetrating life. One could no more tease apart the Spirit from the Father and the Son than one could tease apart the fabric of an atom and still retain the same atom. The divine life is found in the relations of God, in his movements in and through himself. The divine life is dance; not three separate dancers dancing together, but dance, in which three particular movements are discerned within the pattern of the dance-the movements of Father, Son and Spirit.

Thus, the nature of God is found in the particularity of the persons and not in some shared essence. The nature of God is experienced as endless movement and stillness, co-existing. An icon painted by Andre Rublev provides one of the most helpful images of the divine life depicted in this way. The icon denotes the encounter that Abraham has at the Oak of Mamre with three men whom he invites to eat with him (Genesis 18). In the narrative, these figures are referred to variously as men, angels and then as the LORD (the translator's ascription of YHWH, the name of God). The iconographer uses this encounter to represent something of the divine community.

In the icon, the Spirit, denoted on the right of the image as we look at it, defers to the central figure in authority of the Son—for the Spirit always points to Jesus. The Son gazes towards his right, towards the Father, for the Son's love is to reveal the Father and to do only what he sees his Father in heaven doing. The Father, the most hidden of the three figures, holds his gaze towards the Son in love creating a space of intimacy between the two. If we were to draw a circle around the figures we would find that the perimeters of bodies—head, backs and feet—would touch the circle, hinting at the divine reciprocity and endless life-love that flows between the Father, Son and Spirit.

However, this circling love between the figures is not a circularity that is closed. If we were to imagine this meal in three dimensions, around a table, we would find that the fourth side of the table, at the front facing towards the viewer, is open. The icon invites us to conceive of God's openness to the Other as an invitation to come into the divine community, to participate in the divine life.

Drawing on this theology of God as movements in and through each other, we return once more to the notion of God's undefendedness. We see, through this lens, that creation is an act of God's making space for the Other. God, in his self-sufficient movements, withdraws himself, making a space within himself for, and bringing himself in freedom to, the needs of the Other (the world). That which is not inherently in the life of God is granted space by God's withdrawing. Thus, the boundary of the Other, the creation, is respected. Thus, the creation exists within God. It is not that God is within creation as the pantheist would have it, such that the world and the divine are coterminous. Nor is God within us as a kind of interior spiritual centre, beneath or beyond the material to which one day we will return. Nor is God outside the creation, regarding it as self-contained. Nor is God simply holding the creation, actively involved in it. Fundamentally, the creation is an act of hospitality, in which God, within himself, makes space for the other. We find that we exist 'within God'.

To offer hospitality is to offer a kind of space within one's home and self, such that the guest is accepted, welcomed and provided for but not overwhelmed. From their abundance, the host offers a gift that may be received or rejected, appreciated or taken for granted, delighted in or abused. Space is cleared in both the host's schedule and fridge for their guest. Thus, in order to offer welcome and rest the host risks intrusion into their space and home. Hospitality can change the guest and the host.

The creation is an act of God's hospitality. God creates space for the other, filling this space with gift from his abundance but respecting its boundaries. It is a space created by his withdrawal. The movements of Father, Son and Spirit are held back, willingly limited, to allow room for the Other to grow and have choice. The intent is for the Other to say 'yes' to the invitation into the divine dance. It is for the divine dance to be enlarged by the welcoming of another into its movements. Thus the divine life calls. It calls the Other to trust. It calls the Other to an openness in which safety, disclosure, freedom, intimacy, self-giving and receiving are the characteristics of this life.

The divine life also sets the limits of the life available for the Other. In so doing, God himself may be perceived as a threat. But this is a false perception which only leads to frustration and indeed actual death. It is rather like closing one's mouth and attempting to breathe recycled air, air from a closed world where there is no open window. Steadily, this air becomes toxic. Death starts the moment the window is shut—trust is rejected, threat looms and fear enters. Death is a process that only the divine life can overcome.

The divine life limits death by placing a finite boundary in time over the persistence of the Other. Mankind can live three score years and ten but no more. The movements of the divine community choose to tolerate the suffocating spasms of death in the space He has created. Finally, the divine community takes death into Himself, risking the threat of disruption of trust, of love and of mutual self-giving within the movements of Father, Son and Spirit at the cross. Thus, death is taken into the very life of God; the Son cries out in dereliction as the Father and Son are separated. The movements of life and love that are God are broken—death triumphs, putting God to death.

The victory of God in the resurrection is not foreknown by the divine community as an event in the future might be foreknown. That which is within time, on the cross and Easter Sunday, is not played out as a piece within the history of God. It is not enacted as a brief event, before which and after which God exists. Rather, time is within God. The space that God creates within himself includes time. God withdraws his persistent, eternal presence to make space for that which happens in a linear moment. The passage of time represents the chronological separating of the dynamics which are always within the movements of the divine Father, Son and Spirit. Thus, history unfurls, bringing with it an eternal dimension of Otherness. That which cannot not controlled exists perpetually within God.

Thus the redemptive movements of God toward history involve the drawing out of the closedness of this story into another openness. The closedness, the repetition, the self-referential cycles of history in an airless world, are teased open by the movements of the Spirit. Those caught up in this life relinquish the grip they had taken on their place in time and space. They choose to abandon the strategies they had adopted to find life and make themselves safe in a world of self-referential fear. Instead, abandoning themselves to the goodness of the Father, they allow their lives to be caught up in the opening-up histories of God. Indeed, in each and every moment they are becoming more alive. Not that they are finding some essence of their lives, their created identity; but rather, their own dying story, their own dying self, becomes alive, open, whole. Their lives are ones of ever greater openness and movement, of self-giving and receiving. Air re-enters their bodies.

Thus physical death, for these, becomes resurrection. Death releases them from the hostile, closed-in world. Their story unfurls and the beginnings of their lives take wing. The shoots from the roots of their personality, their actions in the world and their creative part in history burst forth into a life of growing abundance. Their identity, rooted in their story on this earth, resembles their heavenly story as an acorn resembles an oak tree. Eternal life is not the stripping away of their personality and story, but the fulfilling of it.

And within God, within the movements of the Father, Son and Spirit, there remains that disruption of death. There remains the wound of the love of the Father to the Son; there remain the scars of the nails of the rejection of Father toward Son, the bereaving of the Spirit, the withdrawal of the divine dance. There remains, in the movements of the eternal dance, a snag, a wound, a stumble, a missed hold, in which the Son falls from the grasp of the Father, in which Spirit perpetually turns away from the agony, but in which the dance is not overcome. For 'I am the resurrection and the life', says the Son. 'For just as the Father has life in himself, so the Father has granted the

Son to have life in himself.' For the divine life which suffered, which incorporated death into itself, which bore the cost of disruption, which did not survive intact, is able to hold within His being the place of the Other which is not resolved.

Thus, we find that to describe God is to describe life that is undefended in its essence. Not a kind of life which has been vulnerable but is now safe. Nor that which has truly risked, but in the end endured. Rather it is to describe life which is always in its essence undefended— wounded, incorporating things unresolved, open to the Other that is wholly and fully safe, which is trust, which is love.

Note on Chapter

Several writers have over the years been seminal for me in the formation of this understanding of God. Whilst he does not use the language of 'undefendedness', Jurgen Moltmann's explorations of the vulnerability of God are clearly influential. With regard to the nature of the persons of the community of God and their interpenetrating movements, Alan Torrance, Colin Gunton, Catherine LaCugna, Bishop John Zizoulas and, of course, John Macmurray have been important partners in dialogue. Without question, however, the thinking of Paul Fiddes, in his several works (listed in the recommended reading) which explore the suffering, openness and limits of God and his depiction of the notion of participating in God, have shaped my thinking. I have chosen not to reference specific sections of these thinkers' books in this narrative in order to allow the description to unfold unencumbered, but their influence resonates throughout these chapters and can be followed up in the recommended reading.

Some readers may detect a relationship between the language in this book and of Process Theology and Open Theism. I do not intend this book as a theological positioning exercise within that wider terrain. However, in broad terms, I attempt to describe the legitimate limits to the openness of God, whilst fundamentally holding out a specific relationship between time and eternity. I regard the relationship described here between the creator and the creator as a form of panentheism (the world within God).

Chapter 10

Living the Undefended Life

*"Happiness is not a matter of intensity but of balance,
order, rhythm and harmony."*

Thomas Merton

To live an undefended life is to join in with the eternal movements of God. One's own movements become fundamentally only responsive gestures to the primary movement of Father, Son and Spirit. This is the life that Jesus himself describes when he speaks of the Son only doing what he sees his Father in heaven doing. What does it actually mean in practice?

Attentiveness to the movements around us

When I arrived at the church in which I was to serve my curacy as a newly ordained Anglican priest, my training incumbent said some profound words to me. They have stuck with me and, increasingly, I think I understand what he meant. 'Simon, when you come into this church, look at the spaces between people.'

He said this in the context of a discussion about the spirituality and godliness of the church—in other words, how to detect whether God was with us and present in our midst. I have suggested that the life of God is constituted in the relationships that exist between Father, Son and Spirit. The divine is not an essence in each person but a quality of relationship between them. This observation transforms how and where we look for God's presence in the world.

We tend to think of such things as the 'fruits of the Spirit' as virtues or core attributes that exist within a person, like an internal ethical guide or a source of energy that leads to godly action. Our minds easily accept the notion of 'essence'; the fruits of the Spirit as an essence in a person's character. But, the notion of an undefended life in God suggests that we should see the fruits not as being within a person but between that person and other people. The fruits of the Spirit are the character of the relational space that individuals foster around them.

The fruits of the Spirit are the spaces between people who are being caught up in the movements of God. As the Father draws the world into the life that exists between Himself and the Son, so the Spirit catches us up into these same movements – the space that exists between changes. Fundamentally, these spaces are no longer shaped by the reality of fear, but instead, by trust. Concealment gives way to truth. Self-promotion gives way to deferral. Conceit gives way to delight in the other. Hostility gives way to grace. Control gives way to service.

This does not mean, however, as I have already indicated, that we become a 'nobody', a mere doormat defined by the dominance of others. Rather, we become courageously and energetically available to join in the missionary movements of the Father to draw the world back into his love. Such movements are endlessly varied. At times, the dance involves pace, energy, drive and drama. At times it slows, becoming still and quiet. At other times the dance is confrontational, bearing strong arms to protect the weak and challenging the dominance of those who would seek to take or abuse. At yet other times, it is self-sacrificing, abandoning power and ceding control to others. At times, the dance is inspirational and evocative, calling people to abandon the familiar and mundane in favour of the radical mysteries of God. At others, it is simple, stately, ritualised, careful and sensitive to the tender needs of the moment.

Crucially, the timing and movements of the dance are responsive rather than directive. The dancer does not determine the dance on the basis of their skill, insights or planning. Rather, the dancer has the fluency and deftness to be able to join in with the movements of God. There is no strategic end to the dance other than the delight and life that is found in abandoned prayer and worship. The impulse to call others into the dance flows from the continued movements of God to reach out beyond that which is already enfolded in the dance to the Other. One could no more shut down the openness of the dance to Others outside it than one could restrict the diffusion of the aroma of a scented candle to the air around it.

To join in the dance of the Father with the Son, through the Spirit, is to join in a life that is abundant, varied, complex, simple, rhythmic and beautiful. It is far from the formulaic and dull kind of life many believe the Christian life to involve. At times, the church has fallen into the trap of formularising the Christian life. Whether this is in the form of rules, codes or principles, written or unwritten, such frameworks deny the responsive nature of the life of discipleship. Joining in the divine dance cannot be codified into a set of steps one can learn and then repeat; they are endlessly emerging. Indeed, the history of the church around the world, through the centuries bears witness to the variety and colour of the different patterns of prayer and worship.

Caution should be adopted towards any single way or structure of 'dance' that is imposed as 'the way' to dance. The old impulse to idolatry is still strong. Any attempts to so describe and then prescribe the shape of the dance in one form or other may come out of a desire to solidify and crystallise the endless movements of the dance. This is not the same as the establishment of traditions or the articulation of some shared behavioural norms. Traditions, if properly understood, represent the sense of rhythm and beauty of God in his movements.

God's movements are not chaotic, anarchic and perpetually novel. Nor are they staid, fixed and closed to change. They have a timeliness and elegance to them, as God moves in conjunction and coordination with the particular history and geographies of the world.

Traditional forms of prayer and worship reflect the movements of God in that time and place, finding responsive form from the cultural and linguistic texture of that community. Like an interweaving tapestry they should not abut one another abruptly and discordantly; rather they should enhance one another by their continuity and difference.

Life as prayer

In this understanding of the movements of the life in God, prayer becomes understood as the responsive posture by which we are caught up in these movements. We sometimes think of prayer in terms of words and communication. Prayer of course involves verbal communication, just as any relationship is fostered by speech—to and fro. However, in itself, prayer is more than the 'conscious occupation of the praying mind'. Prayer is a kind of way of being in the world; it is the posture in which we are open to the movements of God around and through us.

The antithesis to prayer, therefore, is self-sufficiency. We do not cease to pray when we stop verbally articulating words to God. We cease to pray when we cease to move in step with his Spirit. This may also mean that what we count as prayer is sometimes not prayer at all. Many of my prayed words have been an attempt on my part to recruit God to my agenda. Needless to say, I often feel very strongly that my agenda is also God's agenda. Sometimes I am right; I am so caught up in the movements of God that I have a clear sense of what he may be doing or saying in that moment. However, this is not always the case. Sometimes, my praying has the smell of the pagan as I implore a

God (whom I basically do not trust, or think is generous, or for me) to release to me or others what I feel I want or need.

Prayer, then, is a posture that we can inhabit at the supermarket checkout, or behind the wheel of a car, whilst chairing a board meeting or listening to our children recount their day at school. In terms of phenomenon, it feels like a kind of attentive stillness, which allows a committed but non-judgemental welcome of the other. As we experience the flow of life our minds tend normally to be busily making judgments, evaluating our reactions and formulating plans. This flow of words, ideas and thoughts distracts us from the moment and disrupts the posture of prayerful attention. It is difficult to notice what God is doing with such a forceful stream of mental traffic rushing past. Developing a prayed life involves learning how to lessen our attention to this traffic so that the background noise diminishes.

This may start by being able to recognise the ways our minds are 'caught' on a passing thought or feeling. We may be mid-conversation and, suddenly, we have an urge to 'get a point across', 'prove them wrong', 'justify our position' or 'get onto the next thing'. We try to turn the conversation that way in order to get the opportunity to make out point. All the while, our listening to the 'other' is disrupted by the noise of the internal traffic. Meanwhile, a potentially helpful contribution we have to make to the dialogue has been caught on the rushing traffic that fills our mind. The traffic is rushing to the familiar destinations to which our mental roads so often take them and, instead of being open and available to what God may be doing, we become locked into the outcome that road leads to.

In a posture of undefendedness, we are able to offer a contribution that is free and attentive. It is caught, not by our passing mental traffic, but by the movements of God in that situation. This in part, then, involves cultivating the ability to notice and then let go when our thoughts are 'snagged' by our passing mental traffic. The more we become familiar with our historic, patterned responses, then more easily can we notice when they are driving our reactions and choose to let them go. Letting those thoughts go is open to us because we can trust that the Father will, in his generosity, provide all that is needed in this conversation. We are not required to drive some outcome.

So, then, as we choose not to follow those mental tracks, we come back to the person in front of us. We hold them before the Father in our mind and heart, making space to notice their feelings, their tone, their expressions, their words and their needs. As we do so, we choose to welcome them as a friend and to notice how the Father sees them. As our mental noise diminishes, we become more aware of what He may be doing in this situation. This 'wisdom' may emerge quietly, slowly, gently. We continue to listen, asking the Father, noticing our own impulses, cautioning our historic scripts, being open to receive the 'gift' that may be present in that encounter.

As a posture, we seek to be generous, making ourselves available. We seek to trust, not to be overly controlling of the outcome or the return we may get from our investment. We seek to be patient, not hurrying inappropriately to the end point as we try to fit our 'schedule' into our day. We seek to be peaceful, finding the way to understand the actions of the other, rather than stoke the tension by being territorial or defensive. We seek to be kind, responding compassionately to the needs of the person before us, conscious of the way our Father meets our needs in 'the day'. We seek to be joyful, embracing the good things we are receiving in our life as abundant gifts rather than being caught in envy for what others have.

This is the kind of prayed life that the contemplative writers speak of. Those better qualified than I write of it. Whilst there are many different streams of contemplation, they share a movement away from the clutter, plans and strategies of the conscious mind. The prayerful life is not so much a life spent in monastic isolation or retreat. Rather, it is the life lived contemplating the abundant love of the divine Father, moment by moment, rather than being caught by the snags of our defended lives.

Finding the still point

Increasingly, I detect that the 'busy-ness' and preoccupations of Western life are making us search again for the experience of stillness. Stillness is not the same as inactivity or 'rest' as conventionally conceived. Stillness is a quality of attention and awareness inside us, which allows us to move into the world. Some have likened this stillness to the eye of a storm—a point of atmospheric equilibrium right at the centre of a twister. T. S.Eliot seems to be reaching for this kind of image when he speaks of 'the still point of the turning world'—a kind of axis or fulcrum which lies at the centre of all movement.

Growing up playing sport, our coaches would often tell us how we could cultivate an awareness of the game around us such that we were, in our play, never rushed. You see great football, tennis or rugby players seeming as if they have a little more time on the ball than others. Their shots are not hasty, cramped or rushed. This is more than internal composure and assurance on the ball; it has to do with an ability to anticipate the game slightly. Players sense where the dynamics of the game are moving and, intuitively I suspect, adjust their position and posture to anticipate this movement. When the ball comes to them, they are able to receive and welcome it as a fulfilment of their anticipation. They are not playing catch up. This captures something of the sense of elegance and equilibrium which those who move in God are called into.

Yet, many of our actions are attempts to catch up with the pace of the day—to grab the 'almost past' opportunity. Many of our actions are impatient, attempting to force the game, to get it to speed up, needing to achieve more, be more productive. Our movements are hasty, erratic, driven by our own internal pace rather than being elegant, fluid and responsive.

Rowan Williams speaks of an ancient term—equipoise—to describe this kind of posture in the world. It is a term describing balance, where the person is well equally weighted, balanced on their feet. This equipoise gives that individual the capacity of 'ready-response'. In contrast to being leaden-footed, there is deftness and agility, a fleet-footedness, because of the even balance. The person is ready to push off. Such equipoise is available because the world has a movement to it; there is a rhythm, a pattern of movement, around us into which we are being invited.

This movement is 'the day' that Jesus asserts is given to us as gift. This day has its own tasks and work within it. This movement is the 'Spirit' that Paul exhorts us to 'keep in step with'. Again, in 'Burnt Norton' Eliot develops the language of 'dance' to describe the relationship between stillness and movement:

> At the still point of the turning world.
> Neither flesh nor fleshless;
> Neither from nor towards;
> at the still point,
> there the dance is.[7]

Eliot's assertion bears close relation to the understanding of the nature of God as divine movement which I have been exploring in this book. The dance is found in movement. It cannot be isolated into any single element of its constituent parts. It is not found in any one person. This movement has within it its own balance, its own poise—still and moving—a movement that does not send it out of kilter. It is movement that, as one participates in it, renders our experience one of stillness. This movement is the dance of the divine community, flowing into and through each other, into which the Other is called.

Stillness is not physical inactivity; it is not a kind of musical statues. Stillness is a kind of participation within the divine rhythms and dynamics in which our pace is only and ever at one with the movements around us. We are still in relation to the movements of

---

7   In T. S. Eliot, Collected Poems, 1909-1962 (London: Faber and Faber, 2002).

the Father, always moving in time with them, only doing what we see Him doing. It is because of this radical notion of stillness that Maggie Ross can assert that 'Action which does not derive from stillness is mere technique and diminishes those acted upon'.[8]

This is an extraordinary proposition and requires some reflection. Ross suggests that action which comes out of rush, haste, impatience, stubbornness, lust, envy, craving or vengeance diminishes those acted upon. Why? Because it has disrupted the divine dance; it is an impulse and force of influence in the world that diminishes the life in the world. It brings death not life; it closes the world off from the movements of God, rather than opening the world up to them. Actions shaped by anxious fear, or by planned strategy, or by some cause we devote our lives to is 'mere technique'. Why? Because it does not derive its energy and form from the life and movements of the dance. Rather, it is contrived, out of step and wielding its own empty power, attempting, like the artifice of an actor, to convince of its own authenticity whilst in fact being fake.

Perhaps one of the most marvellous, gracious and resilient postures of God is that he nonetheless continues to attempt to incorporate our actions of 'technique' into the divine dance. Who of us can say that much if any of our life has so come out of that place of stillness that it has been genuine? Who of us can say that our movements have ever been deft and light-footed enough to join in with the divine movements around us? At best we are like clumsy beginners attempting to participate in Ballet Rambert. Our movements are crude, unbalanced, dyspraxic and incoherent. They wrench the dance off its pattern and rhythm. And yet, God continues to work with us, to invite us into the dance. He tolerates us, educating and training us, that we might increasingly live lives not of technique and artifice but rather of substance, beauty and truth.

More so, in fact, I believe he reworks the dynamics of His dance to incorporate the forms and shapes we become committed to. God

---

8   Maggie Ross, Pillars of Flame (Seabury Books, 2007).

renders the dance open to change, emergent in form, allowing it to become something in which we have artistic involvement. He does this in his freedom. He does this because, as I have maintained, this is his undefendedness. This is his love. God makes space within himself and his own movement. He incorporates and extends welcome to that which is beyond his control, or, rather, that which he chooses not to control. This is God; He is not overcome by such freedom.

Chapter 11

Spirituality Flowing from an Undefended Life: Gifts, Power and Mission

"By having a reverence for life, we enter into a spiritual relation with the world. By practicing reverence for life we become good, deep, and alive."

Albert Schweitzer

I am often asked what kind of spirituality flows from an undefended life. Are there specific spiritual practices which are consistent with and flow out from this kind of undefended life? Such practices will, of course, also not simply reflect but also nurture and sustain this kind of life.

My first instinct is to say 'the old ones'. I do not regard this language of being undefended as being some novel, twenty-first-century discovery which former generations failed to grasp. The notion of being undefended is not the latest psychological jargon which will be outdated in ten years time, nor does it rely upon insights gained only in certain disciplines in recent years. Whilst I have referred to and related the language of being undefended to some wider intellectual footings and, indeed, the term has its own meaning in some traditions of counselling, I do this not to prove my point but simply to exemplify the wider intellectual coherence of the notion.

I do feel that to seek to live an undefended life is at the heart of what it means to be Christian. And I have no doubt that the best, deepest and richest spiritual traditions in the church have always quested after this freedom. Therefore, there is certainly no particular stream of theology or tradition which has a monopoly of insight into a spirituality of undefendedness, nor any which are bereft of insight. The language of undefendedness is ecumenical and will draw from any and all traditions and the resources they offer to help us reject the fear narrative.

That being said, what are the core elements of a spiritual tradition which is going to foster this kind of undefended life? Whilst it was not my own formative tradition, I am increasingly aware of and drawn to spiritualities which value words not merely as descriptions of reality but symbols opening up a deeper reality. In my own background, which sat within a particular educative context, language was a kind of labelling exercise. To this extent it was always possible to ask if the language was right or wrong, accurate or inaccurate. This kind of discourse birthed the insights of modern science and I do not dismiss the value and benefit in seeking to obtain some objectified description of the way the world works as object. However, what I do reject is the prioritising of this kind of description as a first-order experience of the world.

When we use language to label (to write, for example, about God, or caterpillars, or postmodernism), we risk reducing the world to object. In so doing, we create a distance between ourselves as subject and the other, as object. This distance allows us to create artificial notions of truth which in turn lead to philosophical blind alleys but equally damagingly, they allow us to commoditise the world. This gives us an illusion of control, and detaches us from the risk of involvement. Out there, the world can be known from afar. But it need not touch us. And yet touch is the central experience which humanises us. It is difficult for one human being to be cruel to a baby in its arms, but it is easy for a human being to ignore the deaths of tens of thousands of babies far out of sight and reach. Distance is generally, as I say, a problem.

The same is true of spirituality. Traditions that emphasise the language of God as a kind of objectifiable knowledge run the risk of becoming overly controlling. This is a risk not primarily because they seek to protect the language of God from unorthodoxies, but rather that this language allows them to remain remote and untouched by it. In such traditions, it is often complained that the gap between the head and the heart, whilst only ten inches, is the widest gap in the world. This gap only exists because of an artificial and, I would suggest, false notion of language. Language does not offer us the capacity to 'know something' in our head, such that it does not touch our heart. Nor do we come to know things through the head and then through the heart (as is often maintained). No, language in itself, is a kind of self-disclosure whereby we risk our own vulnerability. It is an act of self gift, by which the world offers itself to us in relationship, and which invites our reciprocal participation. We come to know by opening ourselves up. We can only speak properly of the other when we have first listened to the other. Language is relational and comes from a posture of commitment.

As such, our language about God leaves us in a state of personal dissembling, in which we must continue to open ourselves up to renewal and reordering—in other words, to become undefended. I must be cautious of judging and dismissing your language, and careful lest my own labelling becomes a means of creating a safe world around me. I must be particularly careful of comforting myself in a community which is largely self-referential, where the same set of beliefs are mirrored back to each other and which therefore runs the great risk of becoming idolatrous. Exposure to difference would seem to be essential to prevent the fear narrative restructuring itself in our spiritual traditions.

To this extent, we must also be careful, therefore, of nourishing ourselves with spiritualities that encourage a precise, unambiguous orthodoxy which can be systematised and examined. Whilst we inhabit a spirituality of the Word, this is not the same as inhabiting a spirituality of many words or of a kind of doctrinal word. Our searching for the depth of God is likely to take us to places where we can, in the end, say less about God than we could at the beginning.

In the end, the spiritualities that will lead us more deeply into the undefended life will stop short of easy resolution or confident assertion on this or that argument for God. Conclusions will be reached through struggle and at risk, having spent most of one's time in alien territory, listening to and not speaking the language of the other. That is not to descend, as some will caricature, into a kind of subjective pluralism; rather, it is suggested that the most undefended will always choose to say nothing rather than to defend their stance at the risk of damaging another.

One must equally be careful of spiritualities which encourage the confidence of an endlessly available, personalised intimacy with the divine. Such spiritualities have certainly helped to recover the emotional dimension of our lives which may have been marginalised in the arid conditions of verbal faith. Like any reactive movement they have great energy and appeal. But, also like any reactive movement, they run the counter risk of an equal but opposite questing for certainty and assurance. In this form, the assurance is in experiences of touch, ecstasy, intimacy, joy and laughter. A kind of hedonic high which is equated unambiguously with a divine encounter.

I have a deep and personal conviction that living the undefended life involves experiences of the most profoundly intimate and tender kind. In such moments, our most unnurtured and unconscious areas are touched in the most tender way by the fingers of God. I am not a cerebralist; I am hedonic in that I believe that our greatest rapture and pleasure must be found in God alone. I relish the experiences I have had of such intimacies with God and I eagerly anticipate deeper depths. However, I know too that my divine Father has often times allowed me to struggle with unresolved emotions, even allowing my situations to become bleaker to the point where I could see only darkness. I can confirm that these, too, were experiences of the divine. I can confirm that God was also with me in such times though I could not feel him. I am left, therefore, sure that we must be cautious of either seeking or equating ecstatic highs with the presence and purposes of God. God is present in pain and joy.

Some spiritual traditions, however, tend not to emphasise the intimate highs of God but rather hold on to the unresolved pains of life. Such traditions are usually deeply sensitive to the complexities of the human condition and are unwilling to offer superficial or trite resolutions to our pain. They look with some scepticism at spiritual traditions which assert confidently that God will heal us or give us victory. God is described not so much as the almighty who can transform our situation but as the incarnate who comes alongside us and enters into our situation. The experience of God's life is one of accompaniment more than transformation.

There is something humane about such traditions; they are respectful and mature in their appreciation of the layered and complex realities of human experience. They have perhaps learned to tolerate unresolved emotion and avoid the temptation to tell an endlessly upbeat story of life. However, the truth is that Jesus was indeed raised on the third day. Death did not overwhelm life but it was overcome, incorporated into the divine life. Life is victorious; hope is real. The end of this world is not unresolved but is made whole in God. Therefore, we must be courageous enough to continue to believe in and choose hope, joy and life. If we fail to do so, our energy for change may diminish and we may become turned in on ourselves, choosing not to risk believing in the extraordinary and spontaneous. In other words, our version of the dance may become fixed and predictable just as the dance of endless ecstasy may become predictable.

Gifts and Identity

I have already commented on the danger of equating our skills and abilities with what in the New Testament are referred to as charismata. By their very definition, charismata refer to those things which are given as a gifts in order to benefit others. To the extent that I deploy my skills and abilities toward this end, they are 'spiritual gifts'. To the extent that I deploy them as part of my own strategy of self-protection and promotion, they are not.

That being said, I, like all of us, have cultivated certain strengths and insights through my passage of life which undoubtedly offer particular and specific benefit to others. As I depicted earlier, perhaps one of mine is the ability to think. Now, I acknowledge that my intentions and deployment of this ability have been mixed and self-serving. It has become part of my personality which God is seeking to free me from. Does this mean, then, that in seeking to live an undefended life I abandon my thinking altogether? Should I reject it? Does the undefended Simon Walker have no such 'thinking aptitude'? Indeed, am I suggesting that, if we were all to live truly undefended lives, we would morph into nondescript, undifferentiated entities, or even simply movements, in God, such that my movements could be substituted for your movements without anyone knowing the difference? In other words, do we end up losing ourselves?

That, of course, is the logical conclusion of spiritualities rooted in monism (as opposed to forms of theism), where detachment from self leads to a equating of the one with the whole. However, the notion of self in our undefended proposition is different from this. We increasingly move into the love of the Father as his children. Now, as a father myself, I do not simply love my children 'generally' or merely 'conceptually'. I love my children Barney, Jonah and Olivia. My love is specific. My intention in loving them is that they should grow more fully into their own story of self. I believe my divine Father has the same intention.

In the Father's creativity, the divine dance creates welcoming space for the variety and particularity of the individual person. God's intent is not to flatten out the rhythms of the particular into some general amorphous dance. Rather it is to interweave the movements of the person to enrich the drama, colour, texture and rhythm of the whole. In other words, it involves redeeming our created skills, which we turned to our own ends, by turning them back out again toward the Other.

This is not the same as saying that our skills, once we turn them to Christ's service, become sanctified as gifts. As I have maintained, it is entirely possible for us to redeploy our actions in the theatre of the church (rather than the world) and still be in the business of defending ourselves. Often, the only sure way of relinquishing our personal control over our gifts is to lay them down. To do so truly without expectation that they will necessarily be given back to us is to enter into the journey of Christ in the incarnation. The person who does so, and to whom God does choose to give back His gifts, holds them lightly and for His use. Then, truly they become gifts of power in His hands because they are aligned to His movements of life and not our movements of death.

Power and Leadership

I am endlessly surprised how much is made of leadership these days. Some time ago I wrote a trilogy of books on leadership in which I suggested that leadership is merely the execution of power and the use of influence in taking responsibility for another. As such, all of us 'offer leadership' on a daily basis. The mother at the road-crossing, the nurse administering a drug, the administrator producing a better project plan—all are acts of passing leadership.

Some have rightly noticed that we should talk less of leadership and more of followership—in other words, the things that make people follow the leader. I would want to go further and suggest that leadership itself is an act of followership. There is no such thing as leadership in the sense of executive agency and decision-making that we often take it to mean. The leader is not in the business of taking decisions about the things that happen. Rather she should be in the business of responding to the leading of God's Spirit.

The only kind of leadership possible is described in John 5. 19, where the Son describes his following of the movements of the divine Father. The chief quality of the leader, then, should not be the capacity to make decisions or be visionary, but rather to listen and be attentive. It is startling that we often seek to train our leaders to be better communicators (by which we mean 'speakers') believing that leadership is some act of persuasion. In fact, we should be looking for individuals who have cultivated a stillness of spirit such that they can attend to the movements of God. We should look for leaders who are sensitive to the tone in the room, to the unconscious voices in the discussion. We should be elevating women and men who have an awareness of the spiritual dimension to life that runs in parallel to this world.

I am not in the slightest bit interested in following men and women who can depict some grand vision, or who have a confidence about 'the way we need to be doing things'. I want to follow and learn from the men and women who struggle with the pain in the world and who are generous, kind, self-effacing, seeking to learn, fragile, patient, still and free, those who have known failure and not been crushed. I want to follow the one who can laugh at him- or herself and who does not try to achieve mighty things. As someone once said, 'The immature man seeks to die heroically for a cause; the mature seeks to live humbly for one'.

Mission

Since the seminal work of David Bosch, mission has been increasingly understood not as the recruitment of God to our mission but the participation of the church in God's mission. We speak properly of the mission of God rather than the mission of the church. Bosch's insight is one fully aligned with the notion of the undefendedness of God depicted in this book. Mission is only and ever responsive. The alternative is to be busy doing 'evangelistic things' which are entirely irrelevant to the Kingdom of God. To 'tell someone about Jesus' is not necessarily to bring them the word of life, just as in the same way bombing Iraq from 30,000 feet up in the sky is not necessarily to bring democracy to that country. I cannot but conclude that some of the so-called evangelistic activities that go on the streets of our cities, where people are spoken or lectured at about Jesus, has little or nothing to do with the Spirit.

In other words the form of our mission is itself mission, for 'form' itself is an act of power. If we want to make Jesus known, we must act in a way that reflects the divine life. Primarily, therefore, we must listen and serve. Most evangelism assumes that, somewhere along the line, we must lever in the 'word of God' as if there is some core verbal message that must be 'got across' if evangelism is truly to be said to have taken place. We take this from our equating of the Good News (euangelion) with a divine verbal message. We are conveyors of this message, charged with divine dissemination. We therefore create and take every opportunity to 'get this message' into our places of life and work.

The problem with this is that it prioritises speaking over listening. The result is that we often create a posture where we are telling people the solution to their lives. Few people relish being talked at, or simply being told. Few people delight in the assumption that they have got nothing to contribute to the conversation. Our attempts to allow their conversation are often artificial and slightly contrived– the discussion group in which 'no question is barred'. We have little desire to genuinely 'listen' to the other, perhaps because we do not genuinely believe we much to learn from them. The epistemological conviction lies entirely one way.

However, such evangelism runs the risk of being both indifferent and superficial. God's own evangelism involved the costly commitment of entering into an alien culture. At the very least, therefore, our evangelism must involve our full efforts to understand and enter into the culture we are seeking to reach. It took Jesus himself thirty years before he was ready to speak to his people; we sometimes parachute into cultures from outside and expect people to listen to us within three weeks.

More than this, however, God's own mission involves creating a space within himself for the other. It is, fundamentally, an act of hospitality and risk. God does not survive his mission intact; he is changed by it. This kind of gracious space-giving is a deep challenge to the cheap ways we sometimes try to 'offer' the gospel to the world. When God risks participating in an alien world he incorporates some of it into himself. Might it be the case that we too must be open to being changed by our encounters? Might it be that the flow of transformation is not simply one way? Might it be that we too discover 'gift' from the experience of the Other?

If it is true that God, in his creativity, has woven a diverse and wonderful space in history, rich in cultures and traditions, languages and insights, then would it not be odd if this diversity were simply rail-roaded into cultural homogeneity when it was drawn back into the divine life? In fact, when we glimpse the resurrected community depicted in Revelation 5 we find praise being sung by every tribe, nation, language and tongue. The fullness of worship of God is only to be found when all languages sing God's praise in their own tongue and culture. Therefore, there is a fundamental expectation that there is more to discover and more to be revealed of the beauty and wonder of Christ than has currently been understood—for not all languages and cultures have yet sung his praise.

When I come to the evangelistic encounter, therefore, my ears are open to the way that Christ will become opened up to us both, anew, through a new language. The flow of revelation is not simply one way. The transformation is not only from us to them. Evangelism is, then, always an act of translation and of listening, as many African theologians, such as Kwame Bediako and Lamin Sanneh, have made clear. Moreover, listening is not merely a technical linguistic exercise, but rather a personal and incarnational commitment, which involves creating a space in our heart, mind and will for the Other.

The question we must ask ourselves, when it comes to evangelism, is whether we are willing to bear the cost of sharing the good news. Are we ourselves willing to be truly changed through the encounter, or are we merely recruiting more people to our way of seeing the world in order to feel more secure in a larger population of people 'like us'?

The truth is that mission is inextricably bound up in the undefended life, because the undefended life is always open to that which is outside. It is, by nature, never closed off. As we become more undefended, so we will find ourselves being drawn outside our familiar, comfortable places, to unfamiliar hinterlands and alien territories. Life will be lived always on the threshold. We will both know and not know. Life here is experienced in tension: we are both held, known, secured, and yet at the same time we are vulnerable, pressing into the unknown, listening to the voice of God amidst the lost, dark places of the world.

We are never fully accepted or welcomed, for our posture in the world resists being drawn into the 'club'—the secure, intimate self-referential community of those who all believe the same thing, do the same thing and see the world in the same way. The follower of God is always, in some form, an outsider; she unsettles the settled and yet, at the same time, settles the unsettled. She is a disruptive presence, cutting across the stories the world tells to itself, and yet, at the same time, offering a kind of story which fulfils all others.

This posture prevents the divine child becoming too settled, too attached to any one place in the world. For their destiny is to find their home only and fully in the life of Father, Son and Spirit. To paraphrase C. S. Lewis: God gives us many resting places on the way home, but none are so comfortable that we mistake them for home itself.[9]

---

9   See C. S. Lewis, The Problem of Pain (Fount, 2002).

Chapter 12

Practical Rules:
Sustaining the Undefended Life

"The goal of spiritual practice is full recovery....."

Marianne Williamson

In their book *Punk Monk, New Monasticism and the Ancient Art of Breathing* Andy Freeman and Pete Greig call us to refind rhythms of life in order to sustain our spirituality. What this invitation arises from is a sense that God gives us his world in time, in season, in movements. Like the dancer, we must move in measure within the movements of this world as we receive it.

Learning to dance involves learning how to move in step, in time. Over the centuries, Christians have found that rhythmic patterns of life help orientate and sustain such a balanced posture. Such patterns, or liturgies of life, hold us and prevent us infantilising the present moment as some mere source of immediate, emotional fix.

Any such rhythms, routines or rituals must not in themselves become the centre of the dance. They are not the dance but the movements by which we may be drawn back into the dance. It is likely that they will be coloured by culture and history and that we should beware of imposing them as norms. The beauty of the dance is perhaps in the diversity of movements and gestures, patterns and forms which have been artistically cultivated over the centuries. These varieties of forms enrich one another, qualifying each other so that the dance does not become dull or overly repetitive and closed. They draw us back to the still point within the movement.

The development of a liturgy for one's life, therefore, seeks a way of moving through the world, in time, which constantly opens itself up to the movements of God. We find ourselves coming close to the historic notion of a 'rule of life'. Such 'rules' were cultivated in the main by religious orders to provide structure for community life. They were often enshrined around some central vows which denoted the radical commitment the individual was making to live this kind of life. Poverty, chastity and obedience as in the Benedictine or Franciscan orders represent specific postures with regard to money, sex and authority around which a kind of life can be cultivated.

If we were to extend the fundamental posture of being undefended into three central 'vows' one might reach for the following: Receiving, Welcoming and Stewarding. Receiving expresses the primary orientation of a child receiving the world as gift. It is the antidote to owning the world as possession or exploiting the world as commodity. It is also, one notes, the antidote to 'serving the cause' of God in the way that some forms of Christianity have developed.

Welcoming expresses the responsive orientation of trust in which the other is experienced not as threat but as friend. It does not equate to being a walkover or a door mat. Instead, it seeks to create a hospitable space within ourselves for the other. Such hospitality always, and inevitably, leads us to the third movement – that of Stewarding.

Stewarding is more active that Welcoming. It infers proactive movement to protect, look after and improve the world that we are given. Because we Steward, we seek to preserve those things which are precious. We protect that which is vulnerable. We cultivate that which is growing. We renew that which is being depleted. We seek to give the world back as gift to those who follow after us.

I prefer to read Receiving, Welcoming and Stewarding less as vows and more as movements we are to commit to. When I was an athlete, I would repetitively rehearse the same movements over and over again—jumping over a hurdle till the movement was ingrained, improving my stride pattern until I could every time hit the long jump board from my forty-metre run-up within a centimetre of the edge. Such rehearsal was a mark of my dedication to the sport and perhaps there is a similar dedication required for us to ingrain the movements of Receiving, Welcoming and Stewarding.

Our bodily movements, to extend the metaphor, are largely untrained, and thus our participation in the divine dance is largely unskilled and unrefined. We would perhaps benefit from articulating a set of repetitive actions which pattern this movement into our lives. Once again, such repetitive actions are not 'rules' in that we will be excluded or punished if we fail to live up to them. Rather, they have the potential to draw us deeper into the dance. Like anything, they too can become a substitute for the dance, giving us technical security if we mistake them for the dance itself. But with these qualifications, I have chosen to suggest some actions which may be helpful to us in patterning these movements into our lives.

Movement one: Receiving

...a daily rhythm of receiving at the start of the day before giving
or taking through simple, personal acts of prayer, contemplation,
meditation or praise

...a practice of pausing before taking meals in thanksgiving for the gift to
be received

...a discipline of setting aside time at the start of each new week to
look ahead and receive the forthcoming tasks, work, pleasures and
encounters as opportunities for growth

...a practice of receiving the gifts, fruits and character of each season in
one's consumption of food, one's activities and work

...an annual discipline of beginning each new year with a day (or more) of
retreat

...an attitude of thankfulness throughout the day for the little things in
life that we take for granted (rain, fruit juice for breakfast, a warm bed, a
job, income, family, etc)

...a freedom to enjoy the delights, riches and goods of the world when
they come to us without guilt

...a conscious check on our impatience, frustration or even rage when
circumstances appear to conspire against us

...a decision to try to seek the learning and growth that may lie behind
the difficulties, obstacles and painful inflictions which we have, from time
to time, to endure

...a pattern of planned fasting from time to time (from such things as
television, food, alcohol, etc) as a way of mastering our desires.

Movement two: Welcoming

...cultivating patience and stillness to listen attentively to those we meet so that each person feels heard and not ignored, used or passed over

...resisting the temptation to condemn others who hold different beliefs; rather choosing to listen and understand their perspective and concerns in order to find ways to live as friends

...communicating clearly and authentically the beliefs we, or our community, hold so that it is apparent to others how they can relate to us, understand us and accept us

...developing a commitment to help others understand the impact of their actions and beliefs on those around and themselves, so that they can better take responsibility

...choosing to consider encounters with strangers as potential meetings with friends a gift, rather than a bind

...choosing to be particularly attentive in our lives, our use of time, our skill and our use of money with regard to the vulnerable, dispossessed, homeless and lost in the world

...choosing to welcome visitors, both expected and unexpected, with generosity, and to be willing, as far as possible, to share our home, time and food so that we might bless them as we have been blessed

...choosing to offer back a proportion of our time and / or money as a gift to be given away freely with no stake in the return, as an act of dependence, trust and generosity and as a sign that we are not mastered by greed

...developing a practice of confessing to, asking for and receiving the forgiveness of those we may hurt

...seeking to hand over our anger at what has been wrongly done to us, rather than allowing it to fester and harden into bitterness; in this way seeking to find the will, resources and love to forgive those who hurt us.

Movement three: Stewarding

...choosing to engage in cultivating and creative industry such that our net impact is positive not negative social enterprise, creative or intellectual innovation, authorship etc

...adding to the social capital of our neighbourhood through visiting the vulnerable

...strengthening bonds in our family as a peacemaker

...deepening the relationships we have committed ourselves to so that they are sustained with integrity and richness

...working to protect social structures and institutions which deepen social capital and trust in society and resisting the agendas of those who would exploit the world

...cultivating our own skills as 'gifts' entrusted to us for the good of others so that we can make the best contribution we can to the world

...choosing to limit our consumption of resources energy, food, consumables etc in line with what we need through efficiency, care, self-discipline and restraint

...considering the impact on the environment of our means of transport

...choosing to reduce the impact of our consumption on the planet by reducing waste and packaging and, as far as possible, repairing rather than replacing including white goods, electronics, cars etc

...choosing to consider the origins of our goods and energy, the conditions of those who manufactured them, the impact of the processes and chemicals used in their production (and, as a consequence, switching to renewable energy supplies or buying local produce, for example).

Chapter 13

Diving in

Do you remember when you first learned to swim? You would have been taken to the local pool and, as you got undressed, you felt that shiver of nervous fear and excitement about what lay ahead. First of all, water terrified you! You simply could not imagine how people cast themselves into this huge pool without thrashing around in panic. After all, you had dropped toys into your bath and watched them sink straight to the bottom. And you weighed more than a toy, right? So, stupid, you think I'm going to trust that I will float just because you tell me so?

But, then again, another thought nagged at you...this swimming must be possible, somehow, because...well, they are all doing it! You could see with your eyes the great miracle of other people (fatter people than you, too) who were genuinely floating—simply lying back in the water, doing nothing, and not sinking.

It was the great mental battle between what you knew to be the case and what then you could see was the case. And dividing the two was that old friend...fear. It was fear that held you back from diving in. Fear of sinking like a stone, of gasping for breath and swallowing buckets of water—fear of, well, drowning.

The odd thing about learning to swim is that it becomes harder the older we get. Most things in life get easier to learn as we grow up, but swimming is the opposite. Throw a four-month-old baby into a pool and they will not drown. Rather, a natural reflex prevents them from breathing under water and they can manage primitive swimming movements. For a baby, swimming is natural. They lived in water for the first nine months of their existence. It is their milieu.

I wonder whether living without fear is much the same. I wonder whether we were created to live in the freedom of God's love, like water surrounding us, our embryonic fluid. However, thrust out into the harsh, hostile air of the world, we quickly lose the instinct to swim in love. Instead, we close up, protecting ourselves and learning how to cope.

So, perhaps the journey back to the undefended life is a journey towards our created state. Perhaps it is a rediscovery of our native instincts. Perhaps we are in the business of stimulating old reflexes which we have lost along the way?

The thing about swimming is that you cannot do it from the side of the pool. You can talk about it, think about it and even practice some of the moves, but you cannot begin to do it unless you get in the water. It is the water that makes swimming possible; you simply cannot do it in the air. It is not thick enough.

The same is true of living an undefended life. You cannot do it outside the movements of the Spirit in the world. You cannot do it outside the inside of the divine life. You have to be in the flow; you have to be caught up in the currents of God. You have to choose to get in and then stay in.

Once, a man came to Jesus in the night to find out about the Kingdom.

'No-one can see the Kingdom of God unless he is born again', Jesus declared to him.

'How can a man be born when he is old?', Nicodemus asked. 'Surely he cannot enter the womb a second time?'

'I tell you the truth, no-one can enter the Kingdom of God unless he is born of water and the Spirit', Jesus answered.

Part III

The Quest for the Good Life

Seven Contemporary Aspirational Pathways

I began this book with the quotation 'Maturity is the freedom to live an undefended life'. In the pages that followed, I have attempted to set out why I believe this is the case. However, I have not done so with reference to alternative notions of what 'human maturity' might look like.

As it happens, there are many well articulated versions of what it means to grow into maturity in our society. Each of these offers a vision of what it means to flourish, to live well—related to that ancient quest for 'the good life'.

Their penetration is not limited to just a wider secular audience. There are both Christian and non-Christian versions on offer, some of which have been highly influential. I do not in any way want to knock them down in a critical fashion, for my sense is that each has provided at least something needed in our contemporary culture. In this final section we will consider seven such notions- aspirational pathways to maturity if you like- that are currently particularly influential. The benefit in this is to sharpen the edges of what 'the undefended life' means and does not mean.

Chapter 14

Pathway One: The Balanced Life

Many people see the fundamental human malaise at the present time as one of a lack of balance in our lives. They argue, for example, that we have over-played the function and place of work in our lives. As a result, many of us are stressed, exhausted and constantly under pressure. Our emotional lives suffer, our personal lives suffer and our families suffer.

Some want to assert that we need a healthy work-life balance. Our employers must recognise that we have needs beyond simply earning money. Happiness and contentment is to be found in a balance between a fulfilling work life and a fulfilling life beyond. These elements play off one another—some work, some play, some thinking, some down-time and some creative time make for a whole and healthy individual.

The work-life balance pathway often sits closely alongside guidance about self-management. If we learn how to manage our time more efficiently, to prioritise, to work from our fundamental principles rather than be distracted by things that come along, or have the pressure of a sense of urgency, then our lives can have a basic underpinning of balance to them. One of the most helpful and coherent articulators of this kind of 'principle centred' living has been Stephen Covey whose book The Seven Habits of Highly Effective People has helped millions to pattern their lives towards greater intentional goals.

So, living a balanced life is closely allied to living an intentional, knowing and purposeful life, one which is not subject to, or is not at least driven by, the vagaries of everyday circumstances, but which, rather, has a centeredness or direction to it. Rick Warren wrote a book which asserted that the fundamental opportunity for followers of Christ is to live as purposeful life. His Purpose Driven Life seeks to locate the wider purposes of God as he understands them within the bible, as the compass by which Christians can find meaning, direction, clarity and energy in their lives. In a church which can seem irrelevant and unclear at times, this option of potency and clarity has great appeal. It seems to cut through the ambiguity and uncertainty around us in society at large. Perhaps it resonates, as Covey's book does, with the vivid success stories from the management world—of high-powered executives who, with ruthless determination, focus themselves towards some goal or other. The drive to be high achieving is never far away in a developed capitalist society or indeed in some traditions in the church. So, there is an echo within the balanced life pathway of the call to a effective and productive life; one which is properly organised, clear and effective, and, thereby, achieves more than one which lacks these attributes.

All this is very appealing. There are many young twenty-somethings who, emerging from the indolence of student life, throw themselves with the first flush of youth at their careers only to find themselves submerged under its demands. To find a convincing voice which offers guidance about how to manage such pressures well, without losing the 'fun' of one's lifestyle is reassuring. There are many motivated Christians who also greatly value being given help about how to be more effective, focused and disciplined in their lives and discipleship.

For myself, the writer who offered this kind of voice was Gordon MacDonald in his book Ordering Your Private World. I recall reading this as a student and, for the first time in my life, I heard a narrative of self which took account of me on the inside. I was familiar with books that focused on the lifestyle or behavioural disciplines of living the Christian life but what was so appealing in MacDonald was the search for a centre—the core from which our behaviours come. This ordering of one's inner world before one could order the outer seemed to make basic sense. For MacDonald the balance narrative was played out in terms of the inner and outer life.

Of course, MacDonald himself was, in his writing, reaching for a kind of integrity and coherence that was, in fact, eluding him. His own marital infidelity, occurring at the same time as the writing of the book may seem to some as an archetypal hypocrisy which condemns the book and the author to the scrap heap. I am less judgmental. Often writers are able to speak with power, clarity and persuasion because they know the force of the alternatives in their own being. I believe MacDonald was, in a way, honest in his struggle to order his own private world. His later books perhaps support this. Before I condemn him, I want to be thankful to him for awakening in me a dimension which I have been exploring ever since.

The narrative of balance takes us a long way. In a hyper-mobile, commoditised world, it is certainly a much needed antidote. But can it take us the whole way? Or perhaps we would be better asking the question in another way: does living a balanced life bear the weight of being placed at the centre of God's call to us to freedom in Christ?

Balance, as a metaphor, primarily involves a lack of extremes. A see-saw is balanced when it is equally weighted on either side. Problematically, however, Jesus himself seems to be a slightly unbalanced in his pattern of life. From the Gospel accounts, we are told almost nothing of his first thirty years of life; did he really do no ministry at all in these years? Perhaps so! It seems that the pattern to Jesus' life was one of hidden preparation followed by a brief, intense and even frenetic period of work. As a balance, one could say it is a poor model. Not only this, but clearly there were times of extreme weariness and even exhaustion for both him and his followers during his brief ministerial period. He would retreat, it is true, or pray, and he even took his disciples away to rest; but he then allowed these periods of retreat to be disrupted by the crowds who searched him out. Covey would have been less than impressed.

Not only this, but he was constantly being waylaid by passers-by: women touching his robes, appeals from people for help and children clustering round him. Indeed, not only does he tolerate these intrusions but he also appears to welcome them—asserting, on one occasion, that there is something fundamental about being childlike that is a prerequisite for entry into the kingdom of heaven. Luke, in fact, juxtaposes this story with the encounter Jesus has with the successful young executive city-slicker (the 'rich young ruler') to depict that such self-organisation as displayed by this man plays no role at all, in itself, in the life of the kingdom. It seems that balance or purposefulness in themselves are not what shapes Jesus' life.

Nothing could demonstrate this more absolutely that Jesus' own submission to death. Jesus is hung up for being an extremist. More than that, he insists that those who come after him must also follow this path of radical self- denial. 'Whoever would come after must deny himself, take up his cross and follow me. Whoever wants to save his live must lose it...' It is very difficult to reconcile these words with the call to live a balanced life. It becomes even more difficult when Jesus places some bald alternatives for his disciples in terms of loyalty to him, or to father or mother, children and friends. He promises his followers no secure attachment to place, home or relationship. Indeed, following Jesus seems to be an odyssey of disruption with one's previously well managed and organised life.

The idea of living a 'purposeful life' accommodates better the radical sacrifice to a cause than does the language of 'balance'. However, it also fails to retain the *ad hoc,* impromptu, unplanned and basically disruptive interruptions that continually cut across Jesus' plan for the day. Whilst Jesus could be said to have some central, driving direction in all he did, his subordination to this appears to be far more flexible. Moreover, as the apostle Paul later articulates, God's purposes in Jesus were never to demonstrate power, efficiency and effectiveness. Rather, at their essence, they disclosed the option of weakness and eschewing of 'wisdom'. The guiding centre to Jesus' life was not the fulfilment of a management strategy or the execution of an operational plan. His life and work was purposeful but not purpose driven. What led him was a different kind of voice altogether.

Chapter 15

Pathway Two: The Authentic Life

The second narrative which has become increasingly compelling as a moral aspiration is that of authenticity. We live in a world narrated back to us by a relentless, pervasive stream of media unparalleled in previous eras. As such, one of the fundamental questions which preoccupies us for much of the time is 'Is this real?'

What is real and what is fabrication is not easy to tease apart nowadays. Thus we are deeply sensitive to any detection that the person in front of us is not who they claim to be. Because the media allows such potential for images to be created, manipulated and projected, this task of discerning the truth behind the image is an inevitable and, indeed, right preoccupation. It is one of the prices we pay for negotiating our transactions increasingly impersonally and encountering others mainly by technology rather than face-to-face.

In fact, the question of identity or multiple identities projected through media is deeper than simply being about detecting the fake. It is, more basically, highlighting a crisis in the notion of identity in the contemporary world per se. As Kenneth Gergen wrote some several years ago of this postmodern environment: 'Since there is no essential me, I can be whoever I want to be'.[10] Gergen's point is that the opportunities we have now to clothe ourselves with costumes 'commodiously', as he puts it, allow us to perform ourselves as ephemeral roles, shifting versions of self with no centre,

---

10   From Kenneth J. Gergen, The Saturated Self: Dilemmas of Identity in Contemporary Life (New York: Basic Books, 1990).

no core, nothing to which they are fixed. The self is merely a set of illusions, often incoherent, largely meaningless—a kind of endless entertainment.

Against this context, the call to live out authentic lives has been voiced with increasing passion and weight. In the arena of leadership, one of the hallmarks that people might aspire to is a kind of authentic leadership. By this, they mean one which is not a mere facade. As leaders they are not simply trotting out some party mantras, not merely projecting ideas which they personally do not believe in. What comes out of their mouths does so because it comes out of their core. They lead from the inside out.

Being authentic is about, first of all, a lack of hypocrisy. As a society we cannot bear hypocrites—the trusted MP who is busy claiming expenses to line their own pocket; the bankers using public money to make huge returns for themselves; the financial services industry charged with maintaining secure, well founded economic structures taking calamitous risks with unsecured, overleveraged debt; the priest entrusted with the welfare of his flock abusing children; the 'green politicians' running up millions of air miles and leaving a massive carbon footprint; the celebrities expressing undying love for one another and then stabbing each other in the back. These 'hypocrisies' are a stench to our nostrils and hacks and investigative journalists alike devote vast amounts of time to disabusing us of the lack of veracity of claims public figures might make about themselves.

In contrast, the authentic leader is one who only does or says things that they truly believe in. Like a stick of rock, if you cut them down the middle, they would have their espoused values imprinted right the way through. The British public, for example, took to Vince Cable after the financial scandals and collapse at the end of 2008. The former Liberal Democrat Shadow Chancellor of the Exchequer not only spoke out against the greed of bankers, but had also evidentially appealed well before the event for greater restrictions and cautions.

In his lack of ambition for status, wealth and power in his own life, he lived out the values he called others to follow.

Many of us admire those who we see are 'authentic' in their lives. They really mean it—whatever 'it' is. The lack of pretence, of falsehood and of game-playing is part of it. But also, the total commitment, the willingness to devote oneself to one's way of life speaks of integrity and courage. In a day when most political decisions are made through licking one's finger and putting it into the air to see which way the wind is blowing, such resolute direction is refreshing and inspirational.

We evaluate world leaders through this lens too. Aung San Suu Kyi, for example—the Burmese pro-Democracy leader held for many years under house arrest by the military junta—represents someone willing to pay the price for their beliefs. By contrast, Peter Mandelson has a distinct whiff of the Machiavellian in his endless reinventions, barely taking responsibility for previous derailments before he re-emerges in some fresh incarnation, apparently even more powerful.

So, authenticity is about depth: living a life that matters, has weight and consequences, both for us and for others. It implies true, meaningful and significant relationships in which we are 'true to ourselves'.

However, herein lies the contradiction. By no means does the 'true to oneself' of authenticity necessarily runs alongside a commitment to you, the other. If being authentic is about being true to myself, then I must remain committed to that end whatever the cost to you; otherwise, I compromise my authenticity. Many a relationship has begun with the words 'You make me more me', and has been ended with the words, 'You just don't allow me to be me any longer'. Quite easily the language of authenticity can be co-opted to legitimise our personal desires or fantasies regardless of how harmful they are to others. I know of a marriage in which the husband complained to his wife that his cross-dressing and liaisons with others (in explicit contexts) were just a means of expressing 'who he was'.

What, for example, do we say to the paedophile who deploys the same defence? 'I need freedom to have sex with children because that's who I am?' The discourse of authenticity fails at this point because, on its own, it can have no objection to this complaint. In fact, the notion of authenticity is, in itself, morally blind. It imposes no moral sanction on what is appropriately right or wrong, for right and wrong are determined by whether they are 'authentic' (coherent, integrated) within a person's sense of who they are. On this account Adolf Hitler was a more authentic person than Winston Churchill or, indeed, probably you or I. He lived out his ideology with total commitment and was willing to die for it. Our society might well say of such a person: 'He was authentic in his beliefs, from top to bottom.'

I wrote a book a while ago entitled Leading Out of Who You Are.[11] The title grabbed people because it seemed to chime with this idea of authenticity. Often people would correlate the suggestions in the book with a call to be authentic. When I explained to them that the theme of the book was primarily the dysfunctional damage that leaders do because they (inevitably) lead out of who they are, they were sometimes shocked. It is true, we do lead out of who we are—we do impose our sense of self onto others, conforming them under our own image—but this does not make it legitimate.

The narrative of authenticity is an appealing and convenient antidote to the vacuous, celebrity-infatuated, media-spun world in which we live. It reminds us that a central task in human formation is that of depth and coherence. We are called to be authentic, but we are called to be much more than this as well.

Jesus called many authentic people to renounce or repent of their commitment to their posture and beliefs in life, whether the deeply committed Pharisee Nicodemus, the settled Galilean fisherman Simon (to be renamed Peter), the zealous tax collector Zacchaeus or the young leader whose life exemplified integrity and authenticity. Jesus,

---

11   Simon P. Walker, Leading Out of Who You Are (2007), vol. 1 of The Undefended Leader.

it seemed, was not interested in being authentic per se, but interested rather in that to which one was authentic. Or, perhaps, we should say that he was interested in the person to whom one was authentically devoted. What mattered was not authenticity in itself but rather the kind of authenticity one displayed.

Chapter 16

Pathway Three: The Emotionally Intelligent Life

Most of us grew up under the tyranny of IQ. Some of us took IQ tests which gave us scores, scores which we retained, imprinted on us, probably from that day forward. A firm evaluation of our basic intelligence. A ranking on a universal scale of where we might be placed if all of humanity lined up in a row, the most brilliant at one end and the most dull at the other. For many that evaluation has served to influence strongly the level of self-confidence they have in their academic ability ever since.

One person who was less than convinced of the veracity of the ideology of IQ was the Harvard psychologist Howard Gardner. Gardner proposed that a single dimension of intelligence was inadequate and that human beings displayed multiple kinds of intelligences— from spatial, bodily, musical and mathematical to interpersonal and visual.[12] It was not, he suggested, right to ask 'How intelligent are you?' but, rather, 'How are you intelligent?'

Two of those dimensions have subsequently come to be coagulated together in a term referred to as Emotional Intelligence. Once again, spearheaded by another Harvard Professor Daniel Goleman, the language of EQ (Emotional Quotient) quickly grabbed people's

---

12   Howard Gardner, Frames of Mind: The Theory of Multiple Intelligences (New   York: Basic Books, 1983).

imaginations.[13] Goleman and others set out to argue that people's success in life was as much, if not more, to do with their EQ as their IQ. We had all slightly suspected this anyway; the school boffin rarely went on to make lots of money in the city, or run a successful firm; and indeed many went on to live troubled and difficult lives. Meanwhile, many academic 'failures' seem to thrive much better in the hurly burly of everyday life, with many successful personalities and entrepreneurs having been school drop-outs. It seems that life's broad skills require only a modicum of what we knew as IQ, but lots of other skills as well, including what we now refer to as EQ.

Emotional Intelligence is basically a quotient of one's ability or aptitude against five criteria: self-awareness, motivation, self-management, relationship management and empathy. These five aptitudes are thought to hold the keys to a person's success in managing people. Moreover, they seem to be required especially in management and leadership roles. Perhaps because of this, developing one's EQ has become a goal or aspiration, not just of many companies for their employees, but also of those employees themselves.

Perhaps our interest in this 'soft skill' development makes sense in the context of the history of leadership in the West in the past century. A hundred years ago, few people required leaders of society to exemplify any of these traits. But the catastrophic failure of the leadership in WWI exposed the paucity of authority and respect in which the troops held their officers. Superiority of class, education and qualifications, along with an ability to be autocratic, dismissive, forceful and dominating, resulted in some of the most systemic leadership abuses ever witnessed. A new kind of training was required; a new kind of leader must emerge; a new set of skills must be developed in a post-war world. Many now see the development of their own emotional intelligence as the key to unlocking the higher doors of executive power in their firms.

---

13   Daniel Goleman, Emotional Intelligence (Bantam Books, 1995).

Along with this, the impact of the feminist critique of the second half of the century further undermined any forms of dominating, autocratic and patriarchal leadership. Personal growth was increasingly seen as the developing of sensitivities to another person's viewpoint, an ability to listen without forming conclusions, a literacy concerning one's own emotions and not simply the 'facts' of the case, a basic commitment to working with people as people rather than just utilities to perform functions. In short, for the past forty years we have been pursuing a more holistic and integrated notion of personal and leadership development.

I, for one, am a grateful beneficiary of this gentle revolution. I applaud the work that has been done both to broaden the ideas of ability and intelligence from their narrow base. I am glad to have been able to cultivate a far richer emotional vocabulary which has been instrumental in helping me to become more settled and hopeful as a person. I also weep over the many who have been dismissed, belittled or harshly treated by emotionally illiterate parents, teachers and leaders, and whose spirit has been crushed as a result. There is, indeed, great redemptive work to be done, and we have further to go.

The question is, how much further is that? How much further can this emotional literacy (as I would prefer to call it) revolution take us? Some would want to argue that emotional intelligence represents the next step for us a species and, as it opens out, will provide the vocabulary for us to choose better, more humane and less destructive ways of treating each other and the planet. In its therapeutic application, the idea of emotional wholeness offers promise to a hurting, broken and dysfunctional world. However, to suggest that this alone can bear the weight of the recovery of our societies seems to me to be asking too much.

One of the chief limitations with the emotional intelligence narrative is that, rather like the authenticity narrative, it is ultimately morally blind. Having the ability to treat someone well does not in any way mean that I will choose to do so. Some alarming anecdotal evidence suggests that, for example, rehabilitating serious offenders by developing their emotional ability and sensitivity only helps them further in their abuse. 'Now I know how other people are feeling, it gives me more ways to get into them doesn't it?', has become the testimony of some. Emotional awareness must be distinguished from moral goodness.

The question is: does becoming more emotionally aware have the capacity to make us better people? In fact, despite what I have said above, in general, I believe it does. The reason for this is that, from general experience, when we feel for another person and see them as a person and not a 'thing', it is much harder to do cruel and inhumane things to them. In general, it is distance, not empathy, which causes the greatest inhumanities on the face of the planet. The devastation being caused to our environment and to communities around the world through unsustainable consumption, to families struggling under mountains of debt, to those whose jobs have been lost, is all so distanced from the city executives who, remote and insulated, play with numbers and work out another mechanism to squeeze more out of the markets—and, yet, they are, in some way, a cause. Those same executives do not see themselves as causes of these consequences because they are so distanced from them. As Durkheim predicted, industrialisation will lead, finally, to a state of lawlessness, anomie, because the bonds which bind us to one another, which enable us to self-regulate, will not be present.

So, I am a believer that the emotionally literate life is a better life than the emotionally illiterate one. I also believe that a population living closer, more proximate lives will be more humane, kind, merciful and less acquisitive. Social and emotional proximity does change human behaviour and we must strive for a politics which will engineer this. But, in the end, the reason emotional literacy changes us is because it is a way of paying better attention to the world that is there.

As we become more emotional open, sensitive and attentive, so we become deeper and more acute in our ability to 'hear' our world. We start to hear its songs—of loss, joy, hope and healing. It is not emotional literacy that heals us—it is our world that is the healer—its texture, colour, form, beauty, pain, rhythms and seasons, as well as the community of other human beings around us. This is our source of healing, our garden in which we must cultivate the good life, with the One who creates and sustains it.

Chapter 17

Pathway Four: The Empowered Life

For many, the goal in life is greater empowerment. We live in a world where this language is deployed ubiquitously by government and advertisers alike. Apparently, even my computer has 'empowering technology'. The goal of my local council is to empower residents. My children watch cartoon strips in which the characters 'empower the dragon' (or lion, or whatever).We are, it seems, entirely familiar with the language of giving power to people who do not already have it.

This discourse owes its origins to the influential writings of Michel Foucault who, among others, articulated the archaeology of power as central to the postmodern critique of modernity. Foucault asserted that power always exists in human systems and that the most dangerous kind of power is the unacknowledged kind. Furthermore, modernist societies had been guilty of enshrining abusive, dominating structures of power which denied people freedom, opportunity and choice. The heart of postmodernism as a philosophy has been a challenge to this economy of power.

One of the ways that we experience this most is in the disproportionate affirmation of (most) minority groups. Sensitive to the critique that the majority is always blind to their own privilege and status, political ideology is now instinctively committed to hearing the voices of minorities. The 'goods' in this have been manifold: a far greater resource going towards those with disabilities; attempts to bring women more centrally into leadership in business and the community; and affirmation and support for ethnic groups.

For many, empowerment is closely related to justice. Power is about opportunity, freedoms and choices. Human beings have a basic right to fair or even equal access to such opportunities. The empowerment discourse has indeed set in motion initiatives and agendas focused on alleviating injustice around the world. For example, the international development agendas to which all Western economies are committed, to some degree or other, is universally underpinned by an assumption about the basic good of empowerment. It is assumed that better health care (enabling people to live longer and suffer less) gives people more choice, that better education opens up social mobility and that debt and financial poverty leave people disempowered and unable to make choices for themselves.

For many Christians this broader social, economic and political field has become their primary focus of mission and action. Whereas, perhaps, social reform and action in the twentieth century was motivated by compassion—a desire to help those in need—today the discourse is centred around the fundamental justice of human structures and economies. The passion evoked by globalisation is due to the sense that great forces are at work, shifting, for better or ill, the balances of power in the world. What is at stake is not merely compassion but the fundamental structures of authority and rule in the world. For many this comes as close as anything else to working for the manifestation of the Kingdom of heaven here on earth.

Such conviction of the fundamental priority of empowerment is not restricted merely to macro systems change. It also offers an agenda for personal revolution as well. Most training provided by employers has within it the assumption that the acquisition of better skills (or competencies to use the preferred term) is a good thing. Staff who are better skilled are better able—more empowered—to do their jobs effectively. Underlying this is the central economic assumption that business should exist on a relentless trajectory toward improvement and growth. The current status and levels of productivity are never enough.

Thus, the empowerment agenda has within it two contradictory voices. One is a call for all people to have equal opportunities and access to the same levels of life as others (an appeal to justice). The other voice speaks for continual growth and self-improvement by which individuals and countries with power tend only to accelerate and widen the gap between themselves and those they are seeking to empower. In the end, it results in a territorial resource war, as we will probably witness in the coming decades between the developed nations of the West and the emerging economies of the East. The latter voice ends up defeating the former.

Whilst we can acknowledge much that is good and right about the 'empowered life' agenda, we see that it contains a basic flaw and, as a result, it will never resolve its own internal demands. The problem with empowerment as a central goal of the 'good life' is that it is still, basically, a territorial and competitive vision of human relationship. To empower is to give more power to oneself or others. But for what purpose? So that we / they can better acquire what they want / need / choose in life? Where, then, are the limits? Who defines what I need or what I can appropriately claim as legitimately my right? And how do you adjudicate between competing claims to this or that right when there are not sufficient resources to go round?

The notion of empowerment per se is simply too crude an ideological goal to be workable. Practically, whilst apparently supporting the development of those less fortunate, it actually creates the conditions in which those in power continue to acquire more power. If market capitalism teaches us anything, it is that, just as capital begets capital, so power begets power. Sowing the seeds of the legitimacy of gaining more power as an end in itself is itself dangerous. It is an assumption in modern political life that needs to be exposed and critiqued.

When one comes to the Christian faith, it is far from clear that the God of the bible acts according to this basic economy at all. The apostle Paul, as I have already pointed out, suggests that at the heart of God's movement toward the world is an agenda to overturn the economies of power in society. The cross, it seems, was not simply an act of atonement, but an act of subversion, radically revealing the trajectory of God's own mission agenda—indeed, the shape of the Kingdom. It is far from clear that Christians should be interested, at least at face value, in the empowerment or, indeed, the development agenda at all. The clearest articulation of a theology of God's power in the New Testament is found in Philippians 2 where Paul celebrates the life of Christ as a movement of 'self-emptying'.

Apparently God chooses, willingly, to lay down power in the incarnation—not to deploy the power that is available to him. This has tremendous implications for the church, for Christian leaders and for mission. Some Christian traditions work on the unquestioned assumption that growth is a basic norm in the Kingdom. They take Jesus' mission mandate in Matthew 28 ('Go into all the world and make disciples of all nations...') as an imperative to be continually growing, expanding and moving outwards. In service of this mission, they recruit the most effective, potent mechanisms they can muster to advance the proclamation of the Gospel. We admire churches which have developed impressive, attractive and potent means of communicating the Gospel. We read, with amazement, of churches of massive size—with hundreds, or even thousands, flocking several times a day to fill big buildings. We seek to emulate them and secretly wish that we had at our disposal similar levels of skill, money and resources in our own church. Underneath it all, we have a vision of God as a kind of divine Chief Executive, busily orchestrating an expanding market share of the global population. (Perhaps it is no coincidence that many of these churches are run, or at least financed by, those involved in the financial and banking sectors.)

This paradigm of market share, of growing penetration, of the associated paraphernalia (advertising campaigns, publications, recruitment of celebrities, training of staff, production and commoditisation of resources, and the development of global delivery and support infrastructure, etc) is far more influential in the mindset of most Christian leaders than we would care to admit. The truth is that we are scared of impotence. In the West, Christians are coping with the loss of influence at a public level and the marginalisation of voice in society. For most, the overall experience is still one of decline from the highpoints of social penetration, relevance and influence of a century ago. We are picking over the rubble of once great edifices whose foundations were systematically undermined over the past hundred years. Stories of growth and power are soothing and reassuring to an anxious and dispirited community.

The word 'impotent' is the key word here. It is power that the church feels it has lost—social, moral, political power—or, in other words, clout. In the face of this, the empowerment agenda has been readily and uncritically internalised and legitimised. But, while there are many things we can acknowledge as good in it, fundamentally it is neither successful nor, perhaps, even Christian.

Chapter Eighteen

Pathway Five: The Spiritual Life

For many, the rampant materialism of the West has reached an intolerable pitch. Increasingly, only the most thick-skinned, desperate or outright greedy can fail to see the emptiness, viscosity and sheer brutality of the current versions of capitalism. Without a shadow of doubt, the only remaining ideology that coherently binds Westerners together is a form of hedonism. Indeed, it is taken as read, without question, that the pursuit of a life which is free from pain and contains a good deal of pleasure is to be sought after.

Against this banal, diminished, one-dimensional kind of life, an increasing number are fleeing for richer, older, deeper pastures. Almost invariably, these involve a retrieval of some kind of spirituality. At its most broad this can mean little more than acknowledging the value of things which are not entirely material, visible and monetary. Spiritual can refer to the experience of listening to Hayden, watching a baby come into the world or witnessing a solar eclipse. Spiritual, for many, is synonymous with that which cannot have a monetary value placed upon it.

For some, therefore, spiritual involves some element of the ascetic—depriving oneself of sensory stimulation, making a trek across the Nepalese foothills, stopping having sex of a period of time, drinking only water. These may be routes people are taking to get back in touch with the spiritual dimensions of life. In themselves, they are basically anti-material acts. For others, however, the spiritual can also be acquired. The raft of books on spiritualities available online testify to the consumerism of this lifestyle choice. It is almost as if spirituality can be found among the holiday destinations on travel or lifestyle websites.

Such forms of spirituality have made many Christians sceptical of the depth and reality of the whole 'movement'. They point to the lack of disciplines involved in them; the subjectivity of belief; the centrality of private experience; the syncretism of different world views; the failure to impact on society; and the lack of interest in the poor, vulnerable and unglamorous in our world. In short, there is a critique which sees these forms of spirituality as nothing more than a consumer fad driven by the latest craze to soothe ourselves, fulfil our unmet needs and make our own private worlds more comfortable.

At the same time, it is instructive to look in the mirror of church life and ask: are we in the business of selling the spiritual in the same kind of market? Without a doubt, a large proportion of Christians attend church with the same kind of consumptive, privatised aspiration. People flock to large churches in cities where there is a little mix of class, tone and age to meet with other people 'like them'. For many, the contemporary experience of 'worship' (usually the narrow expression of collective praise-singing) needs to reach a certain emotional pitch to satisfy experiential desires of church. For many, their Christian life comprises lurching from one ecstatic (or less so) encounter with 'God' in a large gathering to the next. To be utterly cynical, one could say the same of the group who hit their acid tabs and ecstasy each weekend in the clubbing scene.

Is God just the legitimate fix? Is he the real deal, the big high who invites us to find our 'spiritual' rushes in him? It is easy to appropriate certain promises of Jesus for this cause. 'I have come that you might have life, and have it in all its fullness.' 'Whoever comes to me will never be thirsty again.' 'If the Son sets you free you will be free indeed.' There is certainly promise in the Gospels that a relationship with God will meet our deepest needs in a way that no other human experience can. This, however, is different from building one's personal discipleship, or the character of liturgy in a church, around the creation / recreation of moments of 'spiritual intensity'.

At the most basic level, we may ask the question 'Is the spiritual synonymous with the emotional?' The psychological experience of 'worship' may bring us the highest, sweetest emotional sensation, but should we equate this with the spiritual? Is the spiritual always pleasurable? Is it always intense? Does the spiritual always take us out of our world into another place?

Or, to ask the question from the other perspective: 'Is God to be found in the difficult, unresolved and mundane? Is God in the dirty, tired and boring? Is God in doubt as well as clarity? Is he is in loss as well as gain? Is he in stillness as well as in dynamic growth?'

The question, therefore, is not whether the spiritual is 'good' but what kind of spirituality is 'good'. And we need to be honest enough to acknowledge that 'Christian' spiritualities can misread the good as much as other forms of spirituality. Dressing events up in the liturgy, costume, language and forms of the Christian tradition in no way insures against such events being profoundly unChristian. More than that, it is entirely possible for experiences in such Christian settings, which have the character of being emotionally intense and high, to be entirely absent of the presence of God. God's presence is not synonymous with emotional ecstasy. He can and will manifest himself in other ways and forms.

Such was the singular lesson that the LORD taught Elijah through his encounter with and subsequent flight from the prophets of Baal in 1 Kings 18. Elijah, the lonely prophet confronts the apostate King and his cabal of idolatrous prophets at Mount Carmel. Empowered by God he demonstrates the rule of the LORD over the other gods. However, the subsequent execution of the same prophets does not spark a mass revival in Israel as Elijah no doubt believed it would. Instead, after this brief act of loyalty, the followers of the LORD seem to slip away again and Elijah is left confronting the wrath of the vengeful Baal-worshipping Jezebel. He flees for his life.

The confused, disappointed and exhausted Elijah is led by the LORD to Mount Sinai, the ancient place of His covenant. There, we begin to anticipate, the covenant promise of God, his commitment to be with his people and to grant them his presence, will be in some way re-inscribed. What Elijah experiences is a succession of physical manifestations of power—the smashing of rocks in a violent storm, the scorching of flames, the thundering of the earthquake. God is the God who has, at his disposal, all the elements—the power to break up, overwhelm, enflame and consume is within him. God is a God who can choose the intense and overwhelming—make no mistake about it. But on each occasion, the text informs us that 'God was not in the wind, the fire, the earthquake'. Instead, Elijah goes outside where he feels a gentle wind and in this quiet, hushed space he encounters his God.

This touch by the divine is, within the narrative, not merely a specific encounter between one man and God; it is not simply that Elijah needed to hear 'the still small voice of calm' amidst his own internal turmoil, as the Quaker hymn puts it. Certainly Elijah needed to learn this lesson; but, importantly, this sits within the trajectory of the decline of faithfulness in Israel and Judah. 1 and 2 Kings tell a story of wilful betrayal by the people and their kings, in the main, of the covenant that the LORD has inaugurated. It is a decline into widespread apostasy. In the face of this, God raises up a sequence of prophets to call the people back to him, Elijah being among the first. The theological question of the day is how will the LORD, the great God who brought his people up out of Egypt, respond to disobedience? Will he come and overwhelm? Will he condemn? Will he destroy? We see, then, the beginnings of the answer in this story: God is fully able to reveal his power and might, overwhelming opposition (Elijah at Carmel), and yet he chooses to eschew such acts of 'shock and awe' in favour of a different mode of encounter (Elijah at Sinai).

This narrative sits within a broader biblical tradition in which God, despite having incomprehensible levels of power at his disposal, chooses, within his own freedom, to limit himself. In fact, as we shall see, the self-limiting of God is not merely a characteristic of his being; rather it is his being. This is the shattering conclusion that the New Testament writers reach as they wrestle for the implications of the life, death and resurrection of the man Jesus. The heart of the movements of God involve a specific kind of vulnerability. This vulnerability is not merely an expedient means by which God redeems his world (Christ dying for us); rather it is the character of the divine life itself. It is eternal life.

The spiritual, if it is a quest for power or intensity of experience, is not in itself a Christian quest. Whilst God can and does offer such experiences of him, they are not what make them Christian. In fact, what is distinctively Christian is the act of vulnerability and self-limiting which is found in the movements of the God of the bible and not in other religious traditions.

I have a number of good friends who seek to embrace a spiritual dimension to their lives but who would not call themselves specifically Christian. One, in particular, is in a position of significant influence in public life and has a number of colleagues who are evangelical Christians. He has expressed admiration for the drive, conviction and energy of those men and women in living out their faith. However, he is sometimes confused and hurt by their attitudes toward him and others. They are essentially dismissive of his spirituality—his practices of meditation and prayer and his desire to find a sense of inner stillness. They are sceptical of his attempts to promote wellbeing and emotional literacy. They are unconvinced about his inclusivism. I have many differences of theological opinion with my friend but I am saddened that, in fact, it is a kind of power and not a kind of theology that separates his Christian colleagues from him.

I find myself wondering whether it is possible to be highly literate and orthodox in one's articulation of biblical faith and, at the same time, to be barely Christian at all. It is certainly true that many who have been given, or claimed leadership, in the church over the centuries and, indeed, today wield a form of power that is little different from a kind of domination. Indeed, for many, it seems only an inconvenience that they are not able to so export the Gospel that the world would be literally 'brought to its knees'. Indeed, there is a casual assumption that this is, indeed, the kind of missionary prerogative that flows from the mandates of evangelism in the New Testament.

Some, indeed, reading these words may be shocked and a little confused that I might be suggesting anything otherwise. Some may believe that I am compromising the very universal Lordship of Christ. My hope, however, in this book is that I have laid out a vision of discipleship that is deeply faithful to the Christian tradition. Indeed, that it might open doorways for a renewed discovery of the depths of our faith.

Chapter 19

Pathway Six: The Fulfilled Life

It seems that, today, everyone is in the process of 'fulfilling their potential'. In the field in which I primarily work, many of my fellow practitioners sell their services under the badge of helping others 'release / unleash / realise / maximise / live up to / live out' their potential. This language, whilst related to the vocabulary of power (potency) reaches for a different kind of aspiration and conviction. It posits that within us there is some untapped well of skill, talent or ability which is to be drawn out through our lives. The vigour with which we are called upon the unleash this unexpressed talent almost suggests a kind of moral crusade—as if it is our duty and obligation to dig out every drop of talent within us.

Sitting alongside this appeal is the comforting notion that we are 'not yet what we could be'. There is more to me than you have yet seen—the best is yet to come; you just wait and see what I could be one day. This is soothing. Depression has been shown to correlate with a low and narrow horizon of future options in our lives. The 'realising potential' narrative suggests to us that there are always more pathways ahead than there were behind us. The future is bright.

Correlated with this voice is also an implicit criticism. Something has prevented (or, more usually, to use the language, 'blocked') our potential from being released. The metaphor is one of a force or flow within us that got dammed up. What stops us being as great as we could be is not some deficiency within ourselves but, rather, the careless or perhaps callous way that the world around has dammed up our gushing river or talent. It is down to others that we have failed or fallen short. The development process, therefore, involves unblocking the resistances that have prevented our true ability from coming out. This may be a lack of confidence, affirmation, opportunity or whatever. Give me the space and a push and my talent with flow.

One of the most influential business coaches from recent years was Timothy Gallwey. Originally a tennis coach, Gallwey realised that what prevented some of his highly talented players from performing at their best was what we call the 'mental interference' which tripped them up. So, for instance, a player might have a slight weakness with their backhand. As they see the ball coming towards them, instead of confidently striking it they fixate on the fear that they will fluff the shot. Their anxious, negative thoughts preoccupy them, interfering with the 'flow' they would otherwise achieve. They fluff the shot and the negative spiral is deepened. Gallwey found that, by a simple mechanism of merely distracting the player from thinking about the backhand they were about to play (by, for example, getting them to call out whether they saw the ball moving upwards or downwards), their shot suddenly and effortlessly improved.[14]

Gallwey's methodology also highlights the other central tenet of the 'fulfilling potential' ideology: positivity. Negative thoughts are considered problematic and destructive. They should be replaced with a positive focus on what we are able to do, can achieve and are good at. Now, of course, there is nothing inherently wrong with focusing on the positive. I myself have at times benefited from conscious affirmation of positive convictions about myself and my life on a daily basis. As a Christian, praise and thanksgiving are central to our posture of worship—and not merely confined to Sunday worship! The affirmation in Genesis 1 that God saw that the world was 'good' remains an affirmation that Christians should continue to make. It is a powerful antidote to cynicism and despair.

---

14   Timothy Gallwey, The Inner Game of Tennis: The Classic Guide to the Mental Side of Peak Performance (Random House, 1997).

Moreover, the creation story is the root of why we can indeed affirm that each individual person has unique and particular gifts within them. Each of us has been created in the mind of God and vested with life as gift—not only in a general sense but also in a particular sense (Psalm 139). God's thoughts for us outnumber the grains of sand on a seashore, we are told; he has pored over us, delighting tenderly and specifically in weaving our frame together. We are art. As such, the expression of the talents within us is always an act of worship to the creator, whether the creature recognises it or not.

The New Testament goes further than this, in fact. As well as the general gifts of God vested in his created beings, God has specially committed gifts, through the agency of his Spirit, to those who are 'in Christ'. These charismata (gifts of grace) are a specific empowering of the church in order that it might be a community able to teach, serve, guard, administer, guide and provide for itself. Many Christians extrapolate from this teaching that they have a duty to 'use' the gifts they have been given and that somehow it would be an offence to the giver of those gifts if they were neglected. The words of the character Eric Liddle in the film Chariots of Fire echo this when the runner explains to his sister that 'I believe God made me for a purpose, for China (mission work). But he also made me fast; and when I run, I feel his pleasure. To give it up would be to hold him in contempt'.

But is this really the case? Is there really an imperative to identify and then utilise the gifts that God has given us? If we have gifts within us unexpressed, then, de facto, we have unfulfilled potential, to be sure; but is God sitting there disappointed that most of us have only accessed fifty per cent of the potential he put into us. Does God have an aspiration for us to fulfil one hundred per cent of our potential?

I am not so sure. For a start, Paul, again, makes it clear to the Corinthian church that any expression of our 'gifts' out of self interest is a complete misunderstanding of their very nature and function (1 Corinthians 13. 1-3). The ideology of fulfilling our potential as a means of self-realisation is anathema, it seems, to living in the Spirit. Paul holds to no notion that, if we have a latent ability, then it is somehow our right or duty to release it. Indeed, he would rather have unfulfilled than unloving disciples (I Corinthians 1. 1-13). God may take an interest in the skills and talents we have within us, but he does not regard them as a means by which we fulfil our sense of self.

Even, however, in the deployment of our gifts for others, the biblical account is far from being straightforwardly positive. There are numerous figures who were gifted from birth (Moses, for example, or Joseph, or Samson) whose stories involve them laying down, or being stripped of, their assets, skills, powers and abilities. Indeed, it is the very loss of these which seems central to their formation of an appropriate sense of self and obedience to God.

And while on each occasion the story resolves with those individuals finally being used extraordinarily and powerfully within God's purposes, their own deployment of their skills is fundamentally changed by their prior life's journey. Moses, a broken prince, pleads for his brother to speak for him. Joseph mercifully forgives the brothers whom he previously belittled and boasted before. Samson sacrifices his own life in one final act of power. It seems that each of them have travelled along a road upon which they have first lost their assets; only through the experience of loss do they come to see them properly not as assets at all but as gifts which it is in their stewardship to use, or not to use, within God's purposes. Their control over those powers has been stripped. There is no sense that Moses would have complained about being unfulfilled had God not used him to rescue his people.

The narrative of gifting in the bible is subtle and has been easily abused by Christians seeking some kind of baptism of a wider discourse of 'fulfilling one's potential'. There is a much stronger narrative in the bible of the journey of loss and laying down of gifts, the letting go of personal fulfilment, the strange discovery of life and freedom in service and even death. God can tolerate us not fulfilling our potential as gifted human beings if it serves his purpose of fulfilling his potential to form us into the image of his Son.

Chapter 20

Pathway Seven: The Sustainable Life

For Christians, the wisdom literature in the Old Testament holds out a vision of 'the good life'. The book of Ecclesiastes, for instance, is an exposition of the writer – possibly Solomon – on the way to inhabiting this world that brings either death or life. Among the themes that the writer explores are many that are highly contemporary and connect with the growing conviction of the need to live sustainably on this planet.

The good life is found in recognising the fragility of one's own existence. The life that leads to death is one that believes hubristically in the power of man to dominate and secure himself. Such wisdom would without question, if embedded in our mechanisms of capital creation and distribution, have prevented the systematic abuses and excesses of the banking sector.

The good life is found in living in time – not as a commodity, but as opportunity and specificity. There is a time for sowing and a time for reaping; a time for laughing and a time for mourning. The life that leads to death is one that seeks to exploit every moment of time, to squeeze the last drops out of it, concreting over the textures of the seasons and creating a twenty-four-seven world.

The good life is found in enjoying what one has rather than continually craving for more.

The good life is found when we make space in ourselves and our communities for sorrow and loss, confusion, pain, failure–as well as for success and victory.

The good life is found not in ever increasing technological and intellectual dominance in which we 'see / record / submit' ourselves to every bit of data available. Rather, wisdom is differentiated from knowledge, and even more so from information, as a way of seeing ourselves within our space and time in the world. Wisdom refuses the enlightenment divisions between moral, artistic, personal, scientific and technological knowledge and invites us into a kind of total participation in the world rather than an observation and commoditisation of it.

It is interesting that, at this time, there is a growing interest in ancient spiritualities based upon wisdom rather than doctrine. This may be a casual and unsustainable distinction but it makes some sense at face value. Many today are drawn more to Celtic forms of Christian spirituality than institutional Roman or Anglican forms. The greater sense of integration of the spiritual with the physical–the seasons, the sense of place and of material, the embodied–feels more whole. Many today are drawn to spiritualities that are rooted in the world and nature as the basic encounter with the 'other'. Many today are looking for wisdom from ancients who had a better regard for the world around them.

I recall with some shame a summer barbeque we had in our garden to which we invited many local friends. Amongst these were a Japanese family we know well. As we tucked into chicken, fish and kebabs, I noticed that the father of the Japanese family declined the plates of grilled meat that were offered round, confining himself to a modest first serving. It got us talking and he explained how, in Japanese culture, one would, before eating meat, give thanks for and to the animal that gave its life. This reverencing of the animal meant that one ate with care and gratitude in an awareness of the cost of the food on one's plate. I was struck by how, despite a historic theology of creation and stewardship underpinning our culture, the West has almost universally come to regard the world as our great bread basket into which we dip our greedy, insatiable hands.

It is no wonder that, in the light of this, there is a profound ethical reaction to the greedy, unsustainable consumption of the West. Nor is this merely political rhetoric. The ecological movement is underpinned, at one end, by a new religious imperative in which the earth per se is seen as demanding our absolute subordination. It seems that, in the vacuum of a spirituality which has sufficiently reigned in the consumption of the world's goods, a new kind of spiritual discourse is being found.

Perhaps one of the reasons why the Christian version of 'stewardship' has had little traction in preventing the West from developing unsustainable levels of consumption is the tension that Christians perceive with our understanding of time. Most Christians see time as a kind of arrow, flying toward the Last Day. Upon this eschatological fulfilment, this world will be 'wrapped up' in some way (whether consumed or destroyed) and a new creation inaugurated. Faced with this inevitable destruction of the planet, there seems little justification in becoming overly devoted to its maintenance. Why invest in the temporary when one should be investing in the eternal?

Many Christians will have in their ears Jesus' own words: 'Do not store up treasures on earth where moth and rust destroy and thieves break in and steal. Rather store up for ourselves treasures in heaven. For where your treasure is, there your heart will be also' (Matthew 6. 20). It seems that Jesus is advocating a kind of deferral of pleasure and reward. The investor puts his assets away in the hope that she will recoup a greater reward at a later date. For some Christians, this motivates a life of self-denial now. I remember in my own story, as a seventeen-year-old, becoming gripped by this idea; that our lives now were the briefest of blips prior to the endless length of eternity. What person in his right mind would trade a momentary kind of pleasure for the kind of lasting fulfilment that was to come? This led me to eschew a potential university education in medicine in favour of studying a non-vocational course and at the same time exploring ordination.

This kind of devotion is predicated on a certain understanding of time in which, essentially, time and eternity have no relation to each other. What is within time now (this world, the planet, our physical bodies, our wealth, what we do here) cannot be transferred into eternity. It will be negated or left behind in some way. The only things that can be transferred into eternity are things which are timeless— things which are not of time. So, 'Gospel work' is not 'of time': telling someone about Jesus is not 'of time' because it will result in the saving of him (or at least his soul) which can continue to exist when time is destroyed. Preaching the word of God, being a full-time Christian worker, acts of moral kindness and generosity—these are all spiritual acts and are essentially 'not of time'. Therefore, they accrue value for us in eternity. These represent what Jesus means when he says 'store up treasure in heaven'.

The reverse is, therefore, also true. Work and actions which are 'of time' cannot be transferred into eternity. Therefore large parts of our actual lives here and now will be discarded and lost. If I were to add up, even at my most overtly evangelistic, the proportion of my time spent doing work which is 'not of time' (in the sense I am describing here), then it would only amount to a tiny percentage of my life. Most of my life—walking to and fro, getting dressed, fixing my bike, organising the finances, collecting the children, sitting on the loo, cooking, sleeping—is irrelevant. It has no currency; it will be lost.

This has always created a great predicament for Protestantism, in particular, and the Western Christian tradition in general. What does God have to say about our lives from Monday to Friday? Does God care what we do? Is our work of interest to him? For many, the only logical answer is no, not really. Some justify their work as a means to 'earn bread' so that they can live and do 'Gospel work'. Others, give the money they earn away to those who are doing 'Gospel work'. Others, by seeing their work place as an environment to do evangelism. Others, by seeking to be salt in their work place, preventing it from being morally corrupt. Others by getting out of the work place altogether (as I did) and doing full-time Christian work (Gospel work). Most regard the Christian life as demanding a kind of witness in the 'world' (work place)—not fiddling the books, not filching from the office stationery account, not overcharging on expenses and certainly not having an affair with your boss—by which one is a 'presence of the Kingdom in the world'.

But, in reality, all of these answers are a thin and slightly unsatisfactory solution to an irresolvable conundrum. If time and eternity are really opposed in this way then the reality is that large portions of our life simply do not really count. It is no wonder that many Christians come to the environmental debate slightly late and with limp heart. They simply see little relevance in it. In truth, all of us should rein in what we consume out of compassion, generosity and self-restraint (it is not good to be ruled by our stomachs), but the idea that the world itself needs to be sustained, preserved in an absolute sense, simply does not resonate. Just as large portions of our lives do not count, the world, as such, does not count.

Some theologians are beginning to tackle the question of time and its relationship to eternity with a little more intent. Tom Wright has written perhaps the most important attempt to rethink some of the significant New Testament passages from which we draw this antithesis.[15] Paul Fiddes has offered by far and away the most subtle and sophisticated exegesis of the theological and philosophical history of these ideas, as well as their treatment in literacy history.[16] Both writers assert that the origins of this myth lie in Plato and the Greek antithesis between time and timelessness. In Plato's reality, the fundamental archetypes of the world exist in timeless reality— beyond time. That which is in the 'river of time' is merely a transitory,

---

15   N. T. Wright, Surprised by Hope: Rethinking Heaven, the Resurrection, and the Mission of the Church (SPCK, 2007).

16   Paul Fiddes, The Promised End: Eschatology in Theology and Literature (Blackwell, 2000).

temporary shadow of the timeless ideal. Anything in time, therefore, does not have fundamental ontological subsistence.

Eternity, in the Greek-influenced Western Christian traditions, comes to be seen as a form of timelessness; for there can be no archetype more fundamental, more perfect than God, and therefore God cannot be of or in time. That which is 'of God' (of the Kingdom) is therefore fundamentally assumed to be timeless—not of the body but of the soul; and the soul will exist in eternity, stripped of the body, and clothed in another body which is a 'spiritual eternal body'. In this way, the Good Life comes to be seen in moral, pietistic ways—the taming and directing of the soul in preparation for the life to come.

We must return later to this question of time and how it intersects with eternity. We will find that it is close to the heart of our exploration of an undefended life. For now, we acknowledge that, if we retain a notion that eternity cannot translate that which is in time into its midst, then we are reduced to a form of spirituality that is ultimately disembodied, moral and pietistic. Moreover, we must say that the Good Life (eudemonia, as Aristotle and Aquinas would understand it) must be teleological. It must concern itself simply with the 'end' for which we are created. And that end, if time is understood as an arrow flying toward this end, is for only a part of us to continue to exist. The Good Life, understood in this way, then must be fundamentally orientated towards the goal beyond this life, beyond this world. It must be purpose driven.

In so doing, however, we find ourselves coming back to the conundrum, which we have already considered, regarding Jesus' own life—the question of whether we can say that Jesus' life was 'purpose-driven'. I have suggested that Jesus did not himself understand purpose in quite this way: Jesus was quite happy to experience time as a moment upon which God breaks in (and hence is willing to be diverted from prior intent and plan to pay attention to the event of the moment). Jesus was quite happy to devote the far larger proportion of his time on this planet to the apparently value-less activities of chiselling furniture and sawing wood. Jesus was quite able to see time and eternity as concurrent, referring to eternal life as a kind of life now which can be lived in the body and in the moment. Not a deferral, nor a withdrawing from this world; rather a way of inhabiting space and time now and here.

Perhaps, then, we should conclude that the Good Life, as we have come to understand it, either in the Old Testament wisdom story or in the New Testament teleological 'purpose-filled, end-focused story', is not quite sufficient to lead us as far as we need to come.

Recommended Reading

The Undefended Life represents the culmination of the better part of eighteen years of study and reflection. Whilst the text is relatively light in citations, the following articles and books have been important in shaping the fundamental thinking upon which the book is based. All books cited are also included here. Please also see the associated website at www.undefended.org.uk.

Barth, Karl, Church Dogmatics (English trans.), ed. by G. W. Bromiley and T. F. Torrance (Edinburgh: Clark, Edinburgh, 1977)

Bartholomew, K., and L. M. Horowitz, 'Attachment Styles among Young Adults: A Test of a Four Category Model', Journal of Personality and Social Psychology, 61 (1991), pp. 226-44

Bediako, Kwame, Christianity in Africa (Edinburgh: Orbis, 1996)

Bosch, David, Transforming Mission (Maryknoll, NY: Orbis Books, 1991)

Bowlby, J., Attachment and Loss, 3 vols (New York: Basic Books, 1969-80)

Brown, James, Subject and Object in Modern Theology (London: SCM Press, 1953)

Covey, Stephen, The Seven Habits of Highly Effective People (New York: Fireside, 1990)

Eliot T. S., Collected Poems, 1909-1962 (London: Faber and Faber, 2002)

Fiddes, Paul, The Creative Suffering of God (Oxford: Clarendon, 1988)

—— Participating in God (London: Darton, Longman & Todd, 2000)

−− Past Event and Present Salvation: The Christian Idea of
    Atonement (London: Darton, Longman & Todd, 1989)

−− Paul, Freedom and Limit (Mercer University Press, 1999)

−− The Promised End: Eschatology in Theology and Literature
    (Oxford: Blackwell, 2000)

Freeman, Andy, and Peter Greig, Punk Monk, New Monasticism and
    the Ancient Art of Breathing (Ventura, CA: Regal, 2007)

Gadamer, H.-G., Truth and Method, 2nd edn, transl. and rev. by J.
    Weisheimer and D. G. Marshall (Crossroad, 1989)

Gallwey, Timothy, The Inner Game of Tennis: The Classic Guide to
    the Mental Side of Peak Performance (London: Random
    House, 1997)

Gardner, Howard, *Frames of Mind*: The Theory of *Multiple
    Intelligences* (New York: Basic Books, 1983)

Goleman, Daniel, Emotional Intelligence (Bantam Books, 1995)

Gergen, Kenneth J., The Saturated Self: Dilemmas of Identity in
    Contemporary Life (New York: Basic Books, 1990)

Goffman E., The Presentation of Self in Everyday Life (Penguin, 1959)

Gunton, Colin E., The Actuality of the Atonement: A Study of
    Metaphor, Rationality and the Christian Tradition
    (Edinburgh: Clark, 1988)

−− Becoming and Being; The Doctrine of God in Charles
    Hartshorne and Karl Barth (Oxford University Press, 1978)

−− The One, The Three and the Many (Cambridge, 1993)

Herrick, Vanessa, Limits of Vulnerability: Exploring a Kenotic Model
    for Pastoral Ministry (Grove Booklets, 1997)

Jones, E. E., and T. S. Pittman, 'Toward a General Theory
    of Strategic Self-Presentation', in J. Suls (ed.), Psychological
    Perspectives on the Self, vol. 1 (Hillsdale, NJ: Erlbaum, 1982)

La Cugna, Catherine, God for Us, The Trinity and Christian Life
    (Harper Collins, 1991)

Lewis, C. S., The Problem of Pain (Fount, 2002)

MacDonald, Gordon, Ordering Your Private World, 2nd edn
        (Highland Books, 2003)

MacFadyen, Alistair I., The Call to Personhood (Cambridge
        University Press, 1990)

MacFague, Sally, Metaphorical Theology: Models of God in Religious
        Language (London: SCM Press, 1982)

MacFague, Sally, Models Of God: Theology for an Ecological
        Nuclear Age (London: SCM Press, 1987)

Macmurray, John, Persons in Relation (London: Faber, 1954)

Moltmann, Jürgen, The Crucified God (London: SCM Press, 1974)

– – The Future of Creation, trans. by M. Kohl (London, 1979)

– – Theology of Hope, trans. by J. W. Leitch (London, 1967)

– – The Trinity and the Kingdom of God (London: SCM Press,
        1981)

Mozley, J. K, The Impassability of God: A Survey in Christian
        Thought (Cambridge University Press, 1926)

Newbigin, Lesslie, Proper Confidence (Eerdmans, 1995)

Nouwen, Henri, The Wounded Healer (New York: Doubleday,
        1972)

Polanyi, Michael, Personal Knowledge: Towards a Post-Critical
Philosophy (London: Routledge, 1958)

Rahner, Karl, The Trinity, trans. by J. Donceel (London: Burns &
        Oates, 1970)

Ricoeur, Paul, The Rule of Metaphor: Multidisciplinary Studies of
        the Creation of Meaning in Language, trans. by R. Czerny
        (University of Toronto Press, 1977)

Rohr, Richard, The Naked Now, Learning to See as the Mystics
        See (Crossroad Publishing Company, 2009)

Ross, Maggie, Pillars of Flame (Seabury Books, 2007)

Schneiders, Sandra S., The Revelatory Text: Interpreting the New
        Testament as Sacred Scripture (San Francisco: Harper, 1991)

Schwobel, Christopher, and Colin Gunton (eds), Persons Divine
        and Human (Edinburgh: Clark, 1991)

Soskice, Janet M., Metaphor and Religious Language (Oxford: Clarendon Press, 1991)

Torrance, Alan, Persons in Communion: Trinitarian Description and Human Participation (Edinburgh: Clark, 1996)

Walker, Simon P., A Brief Introduction to the Theory of Human Ecology (Simon P. Walker, 2009)

—The Undefended Leader (Piquant Editions):

Volume 1, Leading Out of Who You Are, 2007

Volume 2, Leading with Nothing to Lose, 2007

Volume 3, Leading with Everything to Give, 2009

Warren, Rick, The Purpose Driven Life (Grand Rapids, MI: Zondervan, 2002)

Willard, Dallas, The Divine Conspiracy (Harper One, 1998)

Wright, N. T., Surprised by Hope: Rethinking Heaven, the Resurrection, and the Mission of the Church (SPCK, 2007)

Young, Frances, Face to Face, A Narrative Essay in the Theology of Suffering (Edinburgh: Clark, 1980)

Yu, Carver T., Being and Relation: A Theological Critique of Western Dualism and Individualism (Scottish Academic Press, 1987)

Zizoulas, J., 'On personhood', in Persons Divine and Human, ed. by Christopher Schwobel and Colin Gunton (Edinburgh: Clark, 1991)

Other Books by Simon P Walker

THE UNDEFENDED LEADER TRILOGY

VOLUME 1   LEADING OUT OF WHO YOU ARE
VOLUME 2   LEADING WITH NOTHING TO LOSE
VOLUME 3   LEADING WITH EVERYTHING TO GIVE

ISBN: 978-1-907459-04- 7

FINDING THE STILL POINT
52 Reflections
ISBN: 978-1-907459-01-6

A BRIEF INTRODUCTION TO THE THEORY OF HUMAN ECOLOGY
ISBN: 978-1-907459-00-9

THE ECOLOGY OF COACHING
A New Approach to Transformational Coaching
ISBN: 978-1-907459-02-3

WWW.SIMONPWALKER.COM

Praise for The Undefended Leader Trilogy

"Leadership is commonly associated with dominance and power. Simon Walker shows that there are other types of leadership capable of being more effective."
R Meredith Belbin

As Britain's first female Chief Constable, I strongly recommend this to anyone interested in making a real and sustainable difference."
Pauline Clare, CBE

"This is the most important book on leadership I have ever read, because if read and understood, it will change you, to the enduring benefit of those who work for you. My only sadness is that I did not encounter it years before."
Anthony Seldon, Wellington College, Berkshire

"Insightful and helpful. This book is a must-read for anyone aiming to fulfil their potential as a leader. Simon Walker challenges much leadership orthodoxy while providing words of wisdom for leaders who aspire to make a real difference. Drawing on psychological, emotional, behavioural and spiritual theories, as well as his own and others' leadership experience, Simon explores some of the deeper choices leaders need to make. In particular, he highlights the power of courage to help the undefended leader achieve richer meaning out of adversity."
Linda Holbech, The Work Foundation

"Simon Walker's Leading out of Who You Are is one of those unique encounters with an author that can profoundly change how one thinks and behave—about leadership and as a leader. It is having that forging effect on me. I recommend the book to anyone who is serious about understanding their current and potential influence on others."
Thomas G. Addington, Ph.D., Oxford Analytica

"Leadership emerges as a characteristic, in some form, of most people's live. It becomes a means towards human fulfilment in its deepest sense. Seen in these terms, the self-effacing, humble, 'undefended' leader gains a true inner strength. [Simon] offers his insights to a universal audience, as a liberating response to the over-stressed character of so much modern living."
The Rt Revd Dr Peter Forster, Bishop of Chester

"The ideasabout leadership in this book have transformed my self-awareness and I thoroughly recommend every leader to take a close look at Simon Walker's inspired thinking."
Rico Tice, All Souls, Langham Place

"This is a must read for any who wants to understand the drivers behind their own and other's leadership style and then find the way to freedom."
Paul Bendor- Samuel, Interserve, England and Wales

"The Undefended Leader is a very timely publication that cuts to the core of leadership."
Paul Weaver, General Superintendent of Assemblies of God, Great Britain

Visit the web site

www.undefended.org.uk